superfoods

superfoods

EVERYDAY FOODS WITH SUPER-NUTRITIONAL BENEFITS TO BOOST YOUR HEALTH

TRIPLE TESTED

contents

superfood by Dr Joanna McMillan   6

dairy & eggs   8

grains, pulses & nuts   34

versatile veggies   76

super seafood   136

lean meats   174

fruit & chocolate   210

glossary   234

index   237

superfood

While there are many controversies in the world of nutrition, the one thing no one argues about is that the foods we choose to eat have an enormous impact on our health and well-being. Diet is implicated in pretty much every chronic disease that ails us, including the big three—heart disease, cancer, and type 2 diabetes. But diet also affects the way we look, the way we feel, and our ability to perform at our best during work and play. We instinctively know this, and the fact that you have picked up this book is testament to your endeavors toward ensuring you make the best food choices.

Enter the realm of "superfoods." It does seem as if there is a new one touted every week, often on the back of some gorgeous celebrity who names it as one of their secrets to health and vitality. Often the prized superfood is expensive and hard to get hold of, at least until the wise producers get hold of it and ramp up

distribution. Just think of how many "superfood" berries, flown from the Amazon or other exotic locations, or a grain or seed consumed by ancient populations such as the Aztecs or Incas, have become the latest must-have foods in the savvy, health-conscious consumer's shopping basket. All this hype over foods has to make us question what makes a food a "superfood," and are they all they are cracked up to be?

making superfood status

The truth is, there are no official criteria for establishing superfood status. It's a word that has become commonplace in describing foods with something special about them. Usually they are foods that have exceptionally high antioxidant power, or have some unique beneficial plant chemical that we can't find elsewhere. Perhaps the food is an especially good source of one or more vitamins or minerals, or is terrifically

rich in fiber. In essence, while the definition of a superfood is discretionary, these are foods that have some special nutritional attribute to offer us.

our choice of superfoods

The great news is that superfoods are not all exotic products flown halfway around the world. Most of the superfoods we have selected in this book are everyday foods that you will find in your local supermarket or grocer. This is purposeful. While some of the more exotic foods may well have benefits, equally there are many fabulous foods that are produced here in America with proven nutritional benefits that warrant superfood status.

select a powerful team

While there are many superfoods, not one of them has the power to make much of a difference to your health on its own. It is the team of foods that make up your diet that ultimately count. The more different, fresh, healthy foods you have in your diet, the more you diversify your intake of nutrients and beneficial compounds. There are many different healthy diets, but what they all have in common is that they are based on wholesome, natural, minimally processed foods. This book is intended to inspire you to use the most nutritious of those foods to create a mouthwatering menu for you and your family. It's delicious eating, that just happens to be good for you too.

Dr Joanna McMillan
Accredited Practicing Dietitian and Nutritionist

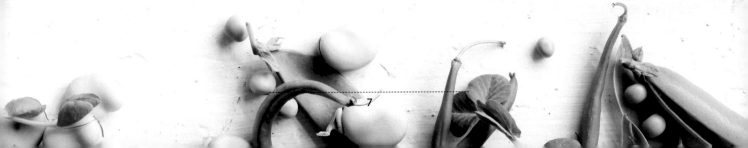

dairy & eggs

Perhaps not the most likely superfoods,
learn how protein-rich dairy and eggs
can help you to control your weight
and boost your health.

This Middle Eastern dish contains protein-rich ingredients: eggs, yogurt, and the seed and nut mixture dukkah. If you eat this for breakfast, it will help to keep your blood sugar levels in check for the rest of the day. And this means you are less likely to succumb to quick-fix snacks.

fried eggs and spiced yogurt sauce

2 tablespoons olive oil

1 clove garlic, crushed

½ teaspoon dried mint

½ teaspoon sweet paprika

1 teaspoon cumin seeds

cooking oil spray

4 eggs

½ cup Greek-style yogurt, warmed

1 tablespoon dukkah

2 tablespoons loosely packed fresh mint leaves

2 whole-wheat pita breads, grilled

1 Heat oil in a 9-inch frying pan over medium heat; cook garlic, dried mint, and spices, stirring for 1 minute or until fragrant. Spoon into a bowl; set aside.

2 Wipe out pan with a paper towel. Lightly spray pan with cooking oil. Heat pan over medium heat; cook eggs for 4 minutes or until whites are set and yolks remain runny. Add yogurt to pan; remove from heat.

3 Sprinkle eggs with dukkah and mint leaves; drizzle with spiced oil. Season to taste. Serve with pita bread.

prep + cook time 15 minutes **serves** 2
nutritional count per serving 38.6g total fat (9.6g saturated fat); 670 cal; 51.6g carbohydrate; 25.7g protein; 7g fiber

tips Warm yogurt in the microwave for 20–30 seconds. Grill pita bread on a heated grill pan or on a barbecue grill plate.

The secret to successful poached eggs is to use fresh eggs. As an egg ages, the white breaks down, becoming runny, and so doesn't cling to the yolk as well. Check the cartons when you buy eggs and select one with the longest use-by date.

poached eggs, portobello mushrooms, and spinach with sweet potato rösti

1 medium lemon

1 fresh long red chile, seeded, chopped finely

2 tablespoons chopped fresh lemon thyme

1 clove garlic, crushed

½ cup extra-virgin olive oil

4 portobello mushrooms, stems removed

2 small orange sweet potatoes, grated coarsely

1 tablespoon whole-wheat flour

5 eggs

¼ cup olive oil

1 tablespoon white vinegar

1¼ pounds spinach, trimmed

1 Preheat oven to 350°F.

2 Remove zest from lemon with a zester, into long thin strips. Squeeze juice from lemon; you will need 2½ tablespoons juice.

3 Stir zest, chile, lemon thyme, garlic, and extra-virgin olive oil in a small saucepan over low heat for 5 minutes or until mixture is warm. Remove from heat; stir in juice. Season.

4 Place mushrooms on a baking sheet. Drizzle with some of the lemon chile dressing; season. Bake for 15 minutes or until mushrooms are tender.

5 Meanwhile, squeeze excess moisture from grated sweet potato. Combine sweet potato, flour, and 1 egg in a medium bowl; season. Heat half the olive oil in a large frying pan over medium heat. Add a quarter of the sweet potato mixture, flatten with a spatula to form a 5¼-inches round; cook for 2 minutes each side or until browned and cooked through. Transfer to a tray; cover with foil to keep warm. Repeat with remaining mixture to make four rösti in total, adding more olive oil to pan when necessary.

6 To poach eggs, half-fill a large deep frying pan with water, add vinegar; bring to a gentle simmer. Break 1 egg into a cup. Using a wooden spoon, make a whirlpool in the water; slide egg into whirlpool. Repeat with a second egg. Cook eggs 3 minutes or until whites are set and yolks remain runny. Remove eggs with a slotted spoon; drain on a paper-towel-lined plate. Keep warm. Repeat poaching with remaining eggs.

7 Heat remaining olive oil in a large saucepan over medium-high heat, add spinach; cook, covered, stirring occasionally, for 2 minutes or until just wilted. Season.

8 Divide rösti among plates; top with spinach, mushrooms, and eggs. Drizzle eggs with remaining lemon chile dressing.

prep + cook time 40 minutes **serves** 4
nutritional count per serving 49.5g total fat (8.7g saturated fat); 615 cal; 23g carbohydrate; 17g protein; 7g fiber

tip If you don't have a zester, you can finely grate the lemon zest instead.

lime and cardamom yogurt
with tropical fruit

2 medium limes

½ medium red papaya, peeled, seeded

1 small ripe pineapple, trimmed, peeled,
halved lengthwise, cored

2 small bananas, quartered lengthwise

1 cup sheep or goat milk yogurt

¼ teaspoon ground cardamom

2 tablespoons oat bran

⅓ cup blanched almonds, roasted, sliced coarsely

1½ tablespoons honey

1 Remove zest from 1 lime with a zester, into long thin strips.
Finely grate zest from remaining lime. Squeeze juice from limes;
you will need ¼ cup juice.
2 Cut fruit into wedge shapes. Place fruit in a large bowl with
grated zest and juice; toss gently to combine.
3 Combine yogurt and cardamom in a small bowl.
4 Spoon fruit mixture into bowls; top with half the oat bran,
then the yogurt mixture. Sprinkle with remaining oat bran, then
nuts and lime strips. Drizzle with honey.

prep time 20 minutes **serves** 4
nutritional count per serving 11g total fat (2.4g saturated fat);
280 cal; 33g carbohydrate; 8.8g protein; 6g fiber

Kidney beans are a great source of protein, complex carbohydrates, minerals, and several vitamins. However, they do lack the full spectrum of essential amino acids—serve the frittata with a slice of whole-grain bread or scatter it with sesame seeds to get them all.

kidney bean, onion, and arugula frittatas with avocado dressing

3 medium red onions

½ pound truss cherry tomatoes, cut into four clusters

2½ tablespoons olive oil

1 teaspoon ground cumin

8 eggs, beaten lightly

½ cup buttermilk

1 cup chopped arugula leaves, plus a handful for garnish

12½ ounces canned red kidney beans, drained, rinsed

1 ripe medium avocado

3 teaspoons lime juice

½ cup plain yogurt

2 tablespoons chopped fresh cilantro

2 tablespoons chopped fresh flat-leaf parsley

1 Preheat oven to 350°F.
2 Cut each onion into four thick slices. Place onion and tomatoes, in a single layer, on a large baking sheet. Brush all over with 1 tablespoon of the oil; sprinkle with cumin, then season. Bake for 15 minutes or until tomatoes have softened. Remove tomatoes; cover with foil to keep warm. Bake onions a further 5 minutes or until golden and tender.
3 Combine eggs, buttermilk, and chopped arugula in a medium bowl; season. Oil four 5½-inch ovenproof mini frying pans with remaining oil; divide onion slices and beans among pans. Heat pans over medium heat, add a quarter of the egg mixture to each pan; cook for 2 minutes or until mixture is half set. Transfer pans to oven; bake for 13 minutes or until just set.
4 Meanwhile, mash avocado in a medium bowl; stir in juice, yogurt and herbs. Season to taste.
5 Turn frittatas out onto serving plates; top with tomatoes, extra arugula, and a spoonful of avocado dressing.

prep + cook time 1 hour **serves** 4
nutritional count per serving 34g total fat (8.5g saturated fat); 499 cal; 19.6g carbohydrate; 24.4g protein; 9g fiber

tip You can also make the frittata in an 8½-inch frying pan; however, you will need to cook the egg mixture in step 3 for 5 minutes or until half set, then bake it for 15 minutes or until set.

If you buy yogurt with live cultures (probiotic bacteria), these have the potential to boost the growth of beneficial bacteria in your gut while minimizing the growth of pathogenic bacteria. The benefits to your health include a stronger immune system with fewer coughs and colds, and a healthier gut.

DAIRY FOODS can also help to reduce blood pressure, and big population studies show associations with lower risk of type 2 diabetes.

BUT OF COURSE not all yogurts are the same. They have different levels of fat, added sugars, may have fruit and other additions, and some are thickened with gums or have other additives. Our advice is to always read the ingredients list to know exactly what you are getting. Your absolute best options are natural yogurts with live cultures, and nothing else in the ingredients list.

yogurt

Yogurt is simply fermented milk, and it probably came about as a method of making milk last longer. In doing so there were unexpected side effects and they were beneficial. Many cultures (excuse the pun) around the world from Nepal and India to the Middle East and Europe have long considered yogurt a medicinal food, and for good reason.

While many people cut out dairy foods from their diet while trying to lose weight, this is quite contradictory to what the research shows. Studies where dairy foods are included as part of an energy-restricted diet show that they promote better weight loss, and most importantly they seem to help improve body composition.

That means they help you to lose fat and keep your muscle—exactly what you want for a lean and fit body. Just what it is about dairy that is responsible for this effect is not fully understood, but it seems to be a combination of the protein, the amino acid leucine, and the calcium that are all found in dairy products.

THE LIVE BACTERIA in the yogurt also helps to break down the milk carbohydrate lactose. This means that if you are lactose intolerant, as many adults are, you may find that while milk irritates your bowels, you can eat yogurt. That's a bonus, as yogurt is rich in top-quality protein, is an excellent source of calcium, and gives you a serious boost in several B-group vitamins, including riboflavin, magnesium, and zinc.

Mushrooms provide B vitamins and essential minerals; leafy Asian greens provide vitamin C, beta-carotene, and potassium, and few calories. Ginger and chile are no slouches nutritionally either; both contain powerful antioxidants.

soft-boiled egg and brown rice nasi goreng

¾ pound gai lan

¾ pound choy sum

½ cup firmly packed fresh cilantro leaves

4 eggs

2 tablespoons peanut oil

6 shallots, halved, sliced thinly

1½-inch piece fresh ginger, cut into thin matchsticks

2 cloves garlic, crushed

2 fresh long red chiles, sliced thinly

¼ pound button mushrooms, quartered

3 ounces shiitake mushrooms, sliced thinly

3½ ounces baby corn, halved lengthwise

3½ cups cooked brown rice

1 teaspoon sesame oil

2 tablespoons kecap manis

1 Cut stalks from gai lan and choy sum. Cut stalks into 4-inch lengths; cut leaves into 4-inch pieces. Keep stalks and leaves separated. Chop half the cilantro; reserve remaining leaves.

2 Cook eggs in a medium saucepan of boiling water for 5 minutes or until soft-boiled; drain. When cool enough to handle, peel eggs.

3 Meanwhile, heat half the peanut oil in a wok over medium heat; stir-fry shallots for 8 minutes or until soft and light golden. Add ginger, garlic, and half the chile; stir-fry for 4 minutes or until softened. Transfer mixture to a plate.

4 Heat remaining peanut oil in wok over medium-high heat; stir-fry mushrooms and corn for 4 minutes or until just tender. Add Asian green stalks; stir-fry 3 minutes. Add Asian green leaves, rice, sesame oil, kecap manis, shallot mixture, and chopped cilantro; stir-fry 3 minutes or until rice is hot and leaves are wilted. Season to taste.

5 Serve nasi goreng topped with reserved cilantro leaves, remaining chile, and eggs.

prep + cook time 45 minutes **serves** 4
nutritional count per serving 18.2g total fat (3.8g saturated fat); 527 cal; 61g carbohydrate; 22.8g protein; 13g fiber

tip You will need to cook 1½ cups brown rice for the amount of cooked rice needed in this recipe.

baked ricotta with grilled vegetables and salsa verde

cooking oil spray

1½ pounds firm ricotta

1 egg

¼ cup finely grated parmesan

¼ cup chopped fresh chives

¼ teaspoon dried chile flakes

5 fresh bay leaves

1 medium eggplant, cut lengthwise into ¼-inch slices

2 medium red bell peppers, cut into eight thick slices

2 medium zucchini, sliced thinly lengthwise

12 slices whole-grain sourdough bread

salsa verde

1¾ cups lightly packed fresh basil leaves

2 cups lightly packed fresh flat-leaf parsley leaves

2 cloves garlic, crushed

2 anchovy fillets, chopped

2 teaspoons baby capers

1 teaspoon finely grated lemon zest

⅓ cup extra-virgin olive oil

2 teaspoons lemon juice

1 Preheat oven to 350°F. Spray a 7¼-inch springform pan with cooking oil spray; line base and side with parchment paper.
2 Combine ricotta, egg, parmesan, and chives in a large bowl; season. Spoon mixture into pan, level surface; sprinkle with chile flakes and press bay leaves on top. Bake for 35 minutes or until puffed and center is firm. Stand in pan for 5 minutes before transferring to a platter.
3 Meanwhile, make Salsa Verde.
4 Spray vegetables and bread slices with cooking oil spray; season. Cook vegetables under the broiler or on a barbecue over medium-high heat for 2 minutes each side or until charred and tender. Broil or grill bread for 1 minute each side or until lightly charred.
5 Serve baked ricotta with vegetables, bread, and salsa verde.
salsa verde Process herbs, garlic, anchovy, capers, zest, and half the oil until coarsely chopped. With motor operating, add remaining oil in a thin stream, processing until mixture is smooth. Transfer mixture to a small bowl, stir in juice; season to taste. Cover surface with plastic wrap.

prep + cook time 1 hour 15 minutes **serves** 6
nutritional count per serving 30g total fat (12g saturated fat); 424 cal; 14.5g carbohydrate; 21.3g protein; 7.4g fiber

Make sure you use a more nutritious whole-grain bread than whole-wheat, which is often high GI, or multigrain, which can simply be white bread disguised with a smattering of seeds and grains.

french toast with poached cherries

4 eggs

⅓ cup milk

1½ tablespoons coconut oil

8 x 1-inch thick slices whole-grain bread

⅓ cup Greek-style yogurt

poached cherries

1 vanilla bean

2 medium oranges

½ cup water

¼ cup maple syrup

½ pound cherries

1 Make Poached Cherries.

2 Meanwhile, preheat oven to 250°F. Place a large wire rack over a baking sheet.

3 Lightly whisk eggs and reserved vanilla seeds (from Poached Cherries in a medium bowl until combined; whisk in milk.

4 Heat half the coconut oil in a large frying pan over medium heat until melted. Dip four bread slices, one at a time, into egg mixture, turning until soaked; drain away excess. Cook bread in pan for 2 minutes each side or until browned and firm to touch in the center. Transfer to a wire rack; keep warm in oven.

5 Repeat step 4 with remaining oil, bread, and egg mixture.

6 Serve toast with poached cherries and yogurt.

poached cherries Split vanilla bean lengthwise; scrape out seeds. Reserve seeds for French toast. Thinly peel a strip of zest from one orange. Squeeze juice from oranges; you will need ½ cup juice. Combine vanilla bean, zest, juice, the water, and syrup in a small saucepan; bring to a simmer. Add cherries; simmer, uncovered, for 3 minutes. Remove from heat; stand cherries in syrup for 10 minutes.

prep + cook time 30 minutes **serves** 4
nutritional count per serving 17.8g total fat (10g saturated fat); 470 cal; 57.5g carbohydrate; 16.3g protein; 6.4g fiber

tips You can use any type of milk you prefer—almond, rice, soy, goat's, and cow's milk are all suitable. If you don't have coconut oil use olive oil instead. Use a gluten-free bread for a celiac-friendly version of this recipe.

Lutein and zeaxanthin have been associated with a reduced risk of age-related macular degeneration and cataracts.

Protein Rich

Eggs provide very high quality protein, with a near perfect balance of the amino acids the human body needs. There's a reason why eggs have been a body-builders' staple for many years. Scientific research is unequivocal in support of higher protein diets for weight control, and eggs are a terrific food to boost the protein content of a meal.

EGG NUTRITION

A SERVING OF 2 LARGE EGGS PROVIDES 138 CALORIES, 12.7G OF PROTEIN, 10.3G OF FAT, AND 1.4G OF CARBOHYDRATE. OF THE FAT, LESS THAN A THIRD IS SATURATED FAT AND OVER HALF IS HEALTHY MONOUNSATURATED FAT—THE SAME FAMILY OF FAT FOUND IN OLIVE OIL AND AVOCADO. EGGS ARE A TERRIFIC SOURCE OF THE LONG CHAIN OMEGA-3 FATS ESSENTIAL TO OUR HEALTH. THESE FATS ARE FOUND IN THE YOLK, ALONG WITH A WEALTH OF VITAMINS, MINERALS, AND ANTIOXIDANTS. SO DON'T THROW THE YOLK AWAY.

The egg yolk is also rich in several essential minerals and trace elements including iodine (often low in our diets and necessary for correct thyroid function), iron, selenium (with an important antioxidant role), and smaller amounts of zinc and magnesium.

eggs

If you're confused over eggs, you're not alone. Once upon a time, before we really understood how diet affects blood cholesterol levels, it made sense to limit foods high in cholesterol. Since egg yolks come under that category, the advice was to limit the number of eggs you ate. Today we know that the types of fat in your diet play a more important role in determining your blood cholesterol profile and dietary cholesterol is far less of a factor. Even if you have high blood cholesterol, you can happily enjoy up to 6 eggs a week.

The yolk is especially rich in the B-group vitamins folate, vitamin B5, vitamin B12, thiamin (B1), and riboflavin (B2). The fat is important as it also contains excellent levels of the fat-soluble vitamins A and E, and significant amounts of vitamin D, along with two carotenoids essential for eye health—lutein and zeaxanthin.

Helps Control Your Appetite

Studies have shown that people who eat eggs for breakfast are less hungry later and correspondingly eat less at lunch.

When you look at the entire nutritional profile, eggs are hard to beat.

huevos rancheros

1 tablespoon extra-virgin olive oil

1 medium onion, chopped

½ pound mini red bell peppers, quartered

2 cloves garlic, crushed

2 teaspoons ground cumin

2 pounds ripe vine-ripened tomatoes, chopped coarsely

12½ ounces canned red kidney beans, drained, rinsed

2 tablespoons coarsely chopped fresh cilantro leaves, plus ⅓ cup loosely packed sprigs

3 ounces feta, crumbled

4 eggs

1 fresh green jalapeño chile, sliced thinly

1 Heat oil in a large frying pan over medium heat; cook onion and bell peppers, stirring, for 5 minutes or until soft. Add garlic and cumin; cook, stirring, until fragrant. Stir in tomatoes and beans; simmer, uncovered, 20 minutes or until sauce thickens. Season to taste. Stir in cilantro.

2 Meanwhile, preheat oven to 350°F; place a 4-cup ovenproof dish in the oven while preheating.

3 Pour hot tomato mixture into hot dish, top with feta; make four indents in the mixture. Break eggs into a cup, one at a time, sliding each into an indent. Sprinkle with chile. Bake for 8 minutes or until whites of eggs are set and egg yolks are just beginning to set. (The cooking time will vary depending on what your ovenproof dish is made from, and may take up to 15 minutes to cook.)

4 Serve topped with cilantro sprigs.

prep + cook time 45 minutes **serves** 4
nutritional count per serving 16.7g total fat (6.2g saturated fat); 324 cal; 19.3g carbohydrate; 19.6g protein; 9.5g fiber

tips The tomato mixture can be made a day ahead; reheat before adding the eggs. If you can't find mini bell peppers, use 1 medium bell pepper instead and cut into chunky pieces.

serving suggestion Serve with whole-grain tortillas.

It's hard to eat poorly when you've got a carton of eggs in the fridge, even if there's little else around. Eggs represent very compact packets of protein and nutrients ready to be turned into a nutritious meal in minutes. Master an omelet, then you can create a filling according to what you have on hand.

mushroom, tomato, and goat cheese omelets

1 tablespoon extra-virgin olive oil

¾ pound mixed mushrooms, sliced (such as button, portobello, enoki)

1 clove garlic, crushed

½ teaspoon chopped fresh thyme leaves

6½ ounces grape tomatoes, halved

8 eggs

⅓ cup water

3 ounces drained marinated goat cheese

1 Heat half the oil in an 8-inch frying pan over medium-high heat; cook mushrooms, stirring occasionally, for 8 minutes or until browned.

2 Add garlic, thyme, and tomatoes; cook, stirring, for 2 minutes or until tomatoes are just softened. Season to taste. Remove from pan; cover to keep warm. Wipe pan clean.

3 Lightly beat eggs and the water with a pinch of salt in a large bowl until combined.

4 Heat ½ teaspoon of the remaining oil in same pan over high heat. Add a quarter of the egg mixture, tilting the pan so it covers the base. Draw the outside edge of the egg mixture into the center of the pan with a lifter or spatula, letting the uncooked egg run over the base. Repeat until egg is almost set. Top half the omelet with a quarter each of the mushroom mixture and cheese. Fold omelet over; slide out of pan onto a plate, folding in half again as it slides onto the plate.

5 Repeat step 4 with remaining oil, egg mixture, mushroom mixture, and cheese. If you like, serve omelets topped with extra thyme sprigs and freshly ground black pepper.

prep + cook time 25 minutes **serves** 4
nutritional count per serving 20.7g total fat (7.4g saturated fat); 287 cal; 3g carbohydrate; 21.5g protein; 2.4g fiber

tip Omelets are best served immediately, but can be kept warm in a 300°F oven for a few minutes while cooking the remaining omelets.

Labne is yogurt that has been drained of whey. A short draining time will result in a thick, creamy yogurt; a longer draining time, like this recipe, will achieve the consistency of a soft cheese, which can be rolled into balls. You will need to make the labne a day ahead.

labne and tomato salad with seeds

You will need to start this recipe the day before.

2 teaspoons sesame seeds

2 teaspoons sunflower seeds

2 tablespoons coarsely chopped pistachios

2 teaspoons ground cumin

1 teaspoon sea salt flakes

¾ pound baby heirloom tomatoes

½ pound truss cherry tomatoes

¾ pound yellow and red grape tomatoes

½ cup Sicilian green olives

½ small red onion, sliced thinly

3 cups firmly packed watercress sprigs

¼ cup loosely packed fresh cilantro sprigs

labne

1 teaspoon sea salt flakes

1 pound Greek-style yogurt

dressing

¼ cup extra-virgin olive oil

1½ tablespoons lemon juice

1 clove garlic, quartered

1 Make labne and dressing.

2 Dry-fry seeds, nuts, cumin, and salt in a medium frying pan, stirring, over low heat for 5 minutes or until fragrant. Cool.

3 Halve or thickly slice some of the larger tomatoes; place all tomatoes in a large bowl. Slice cheeks from olives close to the pits; discard pits. Add olives, onion, watercress, cilantro, and half the dressing to the bowl; toss gently to combine. Season to taste.

4 Serve tomato salad topped with labne and seed mixture; drizzle with remaining dressing.

labne Stir salt into yogurt in a small bowl. Line a sieve with two layers of muslin; place sieve over a deep bowl or jug. Spoon yogurt mixture into sieve, gather cloth and tie into a ball with kitchen string. Refrigerate 24 hours or until thick, gently squeezing occasionally to encourage the liquid to drain. Discard liquid. Roll or shape tablespoons of labne into balls.

dressing Place ingredients in a screw-top jar, season to taste; shake well. Stand at least 20 minutes or refrigerate overnight. Discard garlic before using.

prep time 35 minutes (+ refrigeration) **serves** 4
nutritional count per serving 28.5g total fat (7.8g saturated fat); 445 cal; 29.2g carbohydrate; 13.5g protein; 7.6g fiber

tips You will need 1 large bunch of watercress for this recipe. Labne can be made 5 days ahead. Refrigerate labne, covered with olive oil, in a small shallow container. Drain before using. You can use 4½ ounces crumbled feta or soft goat cheese instead of labne.

serving suggestion Serve with whole-wheat Turkish or Afghan bread.

grains, pulses & nuts

Diets rich in grains, pulses, and nuts
are among the healthiest in the world,
adding years to life and life to years.

The flavors of warming spices, sour/sweet pomegranate, salty cheese, and tangy yogurt all dance happily together in this salad with nutty quinoa. For something different, swap the quinoa for either lentils, freekeh, or barley.

quinoa salad with halloumi and pomegranate

1 cup red or white quinoa

2 cups water

1 clove garlic, crushed

2 tablespoons lemon juice

2 teaspoons ground cumin

2 teaspoons ground cilantro

¼ cup olive oil

½ cup loosely packed fresh mint leaves

3 ounces baby spinach leaves

½ cup sunflower seeds, toasted

8 ounces halloumi, cut into ½-inch slices

¾ cup Greek-style yogurt

⅓ cup pomegranate seeds

1 Bring quinoa and the water to a boil in a medium saucepan; cook, covered, over low heat for 15 minutes or until tender. Drain; cool slightly.

2 Combine garlic, juice, spices, and 1 tablespoon of the oil in a large bowl; season to taste. Add quinoa to bowl with mint, spinach leaves, and seeds; toss gently to combine.

3 Heat remaining oil in a large frying pan over high heat; cook halloumi for 1 minute each side or until golden.

4 Serve quinoa salad topped with halloumi, yogurt, and pomegranate seeds.

prep + cook time 25 minutes **serves** 4 as a light lunch
nutritional count per serving 40.6g total fat (12g saturated fat); 667 cal; 43.5g carbohydrate; 48.3g protein; 7g fiber

tips Fresh pomegranate seeds can sometimes be found in the fridge section of supermarkets. If unavailable, cut a whole pomegranate in half and scrape the seeds from flesh with your fingers while holding the pomegranate upside down in a bowl of cold water; the seeds will sink and the white pith will float. Make sure you cook the halloumi just before serving, as it becomes tough and rubbery on cooling.

Our take on the traditional Italian salad panzanella includes cannellini beans and cheese beefing up the nutritional content with protein, making it more of a main than a side salad. If you like, skip the cheese and stir through a can of flaked drained tuna.

spicy white bean panzanella

5 ounces whole-grain sourdough bread

cooking oil spray

1 medium lemon

1½ pounds canned cannellini beans, drained, rinsed

½ pound heirloom cherry tomatoes, halved

2 Persian cucumbers, chopped

1 small red onion, sliced thinly

½ cup pitted Sicilian olives, halved

1 fresh long red chile, sliced thinly

1 cup loosely packed fresh basil leaves, torn

¼ pound soft goat cheese, crumbled

¼ cup olive oil

⅓ cup red wine vinegar

1 clove garlic, crushed

1 Preheat oven to 425°F. Line a large baking sheet with parchment paper.
2 Roughly tear bread into pieces, place on tray; spray with cooking oil. Bake 5 minutes or until golden and crisp.
3 Remove zest from lemon with a zester, into long thin strips.
4 Place bread in a large bowl with zest, beans, tomatoes, cucumber, onion, olives, chile, basil, and half the cheese; toss gently to combine.
5 Combine oil, vinegar, and garlic in a small bowl; season to taste. Spoon dressing over salad; top with remaining cheese. Serve immediately.

prep + cook time 20 minutes **serves** 4
nutritional count per serving 23g total fat (6g saturated fat); 436 cal; 32g carbohydrate; 18.3g protein; 12g fiber

tips If you don't have a zester, you can finely grate the lemon zest instead. You can use marinated feta instead of goat cheese, if you like.

The carbohydrates

in pulses are very slowly absorbed, giving pulses very low glycemic index values. For example, chickpeas have a GI of 36, and lentils vary according to kind but are in the range 21-42 (low GI foods are those with a score less than or equal to 55). This makes them very good at filling you up and keeping hunger at bay for longer. The result is that you eat less and weight control is easier. The lower GI also means your body doesn't need to produce as much insulin as with higher GI foods. This makes it easier for your body to burn fat, control blood glucose levels, and in the long run, reduce your risk of diabetes.

PULSES ARE PACKED WITH FIBER AND NOT JUST ANY OLD FIBER. WE NOW KNOW THAT PARTICULAR TYPES OF FIBERS PLAY DIFFERENT ROLES AND THE NEW KID ON THE BLOCK, RESISTANT STARCH, SEEMS TO BE ESPECIALLY IMPORTANT FOR GUT HEALTH. THE FRIENDLY BACTERIA LIVING IN YOUR COLON THRIVE ON RESISTANT STARCH AND IT IS THE PRODUCT OF THIS FERMENTATION PROCESS THAT BOOSTS OUR GUT HEALTH AND OVERALL IMMUNE FUNCTION.

There are several characteristics that might be contributing to these amazing effects of pulses. Firstly, replacing some animal protein with the plant proteins in pulses tends to improve blood cholesterol profiles.

pulses

If you've previously thought of pulses as the fare of vegetarians, it's time to reconsider. Pulses include chickpeas, lentils, and dried beans such as borlotti, cannellini, red kidney, turtle beans, and black-eyed peas. These pack a pretty powerful nutritional punch, being rich in plant protein, providing slow release, low-GI carbohydrates, stacks of fiber and a wealth of vitamins, minerals, and beneficial plant chemicals.

Eating more pulses might also help you to live longer. A study of older people from varying dietary cultures, including Australia, Japan, Sweden, and Greece, found that intake of pulses was the strongest dietary predictor of survival. Who knew that such a humble food group could have such a powerful effect on health? In fact, for every additional 20g of pulses consumed, the risk of death was 7-8 percent lower.

Pulses are high-ranking players when it comes to beneficial plant compounds. They contain a wealth of phytochemicals that have been shown to benefit our health, including phytosterols, isoflavones, saponins, alkaloids, and phytates.

While phytates have received some bad press mostly on account of their ability to bind minerals such as iron, lowering their absorption, overall phytates have been associated with beneficial effects. By consuming a varied diet with plenty of foods rich in minerals, you needn't worry about the small amounts that may be caught up with phytates.

miso almond veggie patties

2 tablespoons white (shiro) miso

2 tablespoons sesame seeds, roasted

1 cup almonds, roasted

4 tablespoons vegetable oil

2 green onions (scallions), chopped

5½ ounces cremini mushrooms, chopped coarsely

1 tablespoon light soy sauce

1 teaspoon Chinese five-spice powder

2 teaspoons honey

½ cup panko (Japanese) breadcrumbs

1 egg, beaten lightly

½ cup mayonnaise

2 teaspoons lime juice

1 lime, cut into wedges

pickled cabbage salad

14½ ounces red cabbage, shredded finely

2 green onions (scallions), sliced thinly

4 radishes, sliced thinly

1 tablespoon chopped pickled ginger

2 tablespoons lime juice

2 tablespoons rice wine vinegar

1 tablespoon light soy sauce

1 teaspoon caster (superfine) sugar

1 Make Pickled Cabbage Salad.

2 Process miso, seeds, and nuts until roughly combined; leave mixture in processor.

3 Heat half the oil in a large frying pan over medium heat; cook onion and mushrooms for 3 minutes or until browned. Add sauce and five spice; cook for 30 seconds. Add mushroom mixture to processor with honey, breadcrumbs, and egg; pulse until well combined but not smooth. Shape 1½ tablespoons of the mixture into 12 patties.

4 Heat half the remaining oil in a large frying pan over medium heat; cook patties, in three batches, 2 minutes each side or until golden, adding remaining oil in between batches.

5 Combine mayonnaise and juice in a small bowl.

6 Serve patties with Pickled Cabbage Salad, lime mayonnaise, and lime wedges.

pickled cabbage salad Place cabbage, onion, radish, and ginger in a large bowl. Pour combined juice, vinegar, sauce, and sugar over salad; toss gently to combine.

prep + cook time 30 minutes **serves** 4
nutritional count per serving 59.2g total fat (6.2g saturated fat); 736 cal; 27g carbohydrate; 19.4g protein; 10.6g fiber

tip You can form the mixture into four burger patties, then serve with mayonnaise and cabbage salad in whole-wheat buns.

rosemary and tomato
barley risotto with mozzarella

1 tablespoon olive oil

1 small onion, chopped finely

2 cloves garlic, crushed

1 medium red bell pepper, sliced

1 tablespoon fresh rosemary, chopped finely

1½ cups pearl barley

5 cups vegetable stock

12½ ounces canned diced tomatoes

1 cup bottled tomato passata

2 teaspoons caster sugar

2 teaspoons finely grated lemon zest

6½ ounces buffalo mozzarella, torn

1 tablespoon chile-infused olive oil

½ cup loosely packed fresh flat-leaf parsley leaves

1 Heat olive oil in a large saucepan over medium heat; cook onion, garlic, bell pepper, and rosemary for 5 minutes or until tender.

2 Add barley; cook, stirring, for 1 minute. Add stock, tomatoes, passata, sugar, and zest; bring to a boil. Reduce heat to low; cook, stirring occasionally, for 45 minutes or until barley is tender. Season to taste.

3 Spoon risotto into bowls; top with mozzarella, drizzle with chile oil, and sprinkle with parsley.

prep + cook time 55 minutes **serves** 4

nutritional count per serving 24.5g total fat (9.2g saturated fat); 592 cal; 61.6g carbohydrate; 24.8g protein; 13.7g fiber

tips You could also use large balls of fresh cow's milk mozzarella, which are known as fior di latte—literally meaning "flower of the milk". Use a pinch of chile flakes or a little chopped fresh chile and extra-virgin olive oil instead of the chile-infused oil. Passata is pureed and sieved Italian tomatoes and is available from supermarkets.

spiced chickpea and cauliflower dosa

3½ tablespoons vegetable oil

1 large onion, chopped finely

2 cloves garlic, crushed

2 teaspoons cumin seeds

1½-inch piece fresh ginger, grated finely

1 tablespoon Indian curry powder

2 teaspoons yellow mustard seeds

1 pound cauliflower, cut into small florets

12½ ounces canned chickpeas, drained, rinsed

1 cup vegetable stock

1½ tablespoons vegetable oil, extra

3 limes, halved

½ cup loosely packed fresh cilantro leaves

cucumber yogurt

1 cup Greek-style yogurt

1 Persian cucumber, grated coarsely

1 teaspoon dried mint

dosa batter

1 cup chickpea flour (besan)

1 cup all-purpose flour

1 teaspoon ground cumin

½ teaspoon baking soda

¼ teaspoon sea salt flakes

2 cups cold tap water

1 Heat 2 tablespoons oil in a large frying pan over medium heat; cook onion, garlic, cumin, ginger, curry powder, and mustard seeds for 5 minutes or until onion is soft. Add cauliflower and chickpeas; cook, stirring, for 2 minutes. Add stock; cook, partially covered, for 15 minutes or until cauliflower is tender. Roughly mash cauliflower and chickpeas with the back of a spoon. Season to taste. Set aside; keep warm.

2 Make Cucumber Yogurt.

3 Make Dosa Batter.

4 Heat 1 teaspoon oil in a 10-inch frying pan over medium heat. Add ½ cup of batter and quickly spread with a metal spatula to cover the base; cook 2 minutes or until mixture bubbles. Top with one-sixth of the cauliflower mixture; cook a further 2 minutes or until base is crisp and golden. Roll up dosa to enclose filling; slide onto a plate. Repeat with remaining oil, batter, and cauliflower mixture to make six dosas in total.

5 Serve dosas with cucumber yogurt and lime halves, scattered with cilantro.

cucumber yogurt Combine ingredients in a medium bowl. Season to taste.

dosa batter Sift flours, cumin, baking soda, and salt into a bowl. Whisk in the water until combined.

prep + cook time 45 minutes makes 6
nutritional count per dosa 17.3g total fat (3.5g saturated fat); 436 cal; 51g carbohydrate; 14.3g protein; 8.2g fiber

tips Chickpea flour (besan) is available from the health food aisle of supermarkets or health food stores. Keep dosas warm in a preheated 350°F oven in between batches.

Sunflower seeds

are one of the richest sources of vitamin E, with a tablespoon of seeds providing 22% of what experts calculate women need in a day, and 16% for men. Vitamin E is the chief fat-soluble antioxidant in the body, and plays a crucial role in protecting cells from damage, including sun damage to the skin. That's one reason why you'll find vitamin E in so many face creams, but you want to make sure you feed your skin from the inside out too.

Pumpkin seeds are an excellent source of magnesium, needed for more than 300 biochemical reactions in the body. You need it for a healthy immune system, to keep your blood pressure where it should be, for normal muscle and nerve function, to manage blood glucose levels, and to keep your bones strong.

Quinoa is rich in several B-group vitamins required to turn the food you eat into energy to fuel your body. A serve of quinoa will provide you with folate, thiamin, riboflavin, vitamin B6 and smaller amounts of niacin.

FLAXSEED IS ESPECIALLY

RICH IN FIBER. ADDING JUST A TABLESPOON TO YOUR BREAKFAST DELIVERS AN EXTRA 3G OF FIBER. FLAXSEED, ALONG WITH CHIA, IS A STAND-OUT AMONGT SEEDS AS BEING ONE OF THE HIGHEST SOURCES OF PLANT OMEGA-3 FATS. WHILE THESE ARE NOT QUITE THE SAME AS THE LONG CHAIN OMEGA-3s FOUND IN OILY FISH, THEY ARE BENEFICIAL NONETHELESS AND PLAY AN ANTI-INFLAMMATORY ROLE IN THE BODY.

seeds & quinoa

Quinoa (pronounced keen-wa) is cooked and eaten as a grain alternative, but it is in fact a seed. You'll often hear it called a pseudo-grain for that reason, similar to amaranth. While it might be relatively new to many of us, quinoa has been a staple food for thousands of years in the Andean region of South America. The Incas reportedly considered it sacred, calling it "the mother of all grains".

Seeds are the means by which many plants procreate. The seed must therefore give the new seedling the nutrition it needs to sprout and grow. That's why they are such nutritional powerhouses. They provide good quality protein, providing all of the essential amino acids, making them an especially good addition to a vegetarian meal. You'll find a wealth of antioxidants and other beneficial plant compounds, many unique to seeds.

The oldest living person in the world (at the time of writing) is a 123-year-old Bolivian farmer. He attributes his long life, free of any serious illness, to his traditional Andean diet, with quinoa as a staple food.

A STUDY OF over 5,000 Finnish adults, followed for 14 years, found that those with higher vitamin E intakes from food were significantly less likely to die from heart disease.

Quinoa earns superfood status as it boasts an impressive nutritional profile. It has double the protein of rice and provides all of the essential amino acids—the building blocks of protein.

indian-spiced quinoa cakes with tomatoes

¾ pound orange sweet potato, peeled, cut into 1½-inch cubes

2 cups water

1 cup white quinoa

⅓ cup plus 1 tablespoon olive oil

1 medium onion, chopped finely

2 cloves garlic, crushed

1½-inch piece fresh ginger, grated finely

1 fresh long red chile, chopped finely

1½ tablespoons Indian curry powder

⅓ cup chopped fresh cilantro

1 egg

¼ cup whole-wheat flour

1 pound Roma tomatoes, each cut into 6 wedges

1 tablespoon yellow mustard seeds

2 tablespoons fresh curry leaves

⅔ cup Greek-style yogurt

2 cups baby Asian salad leaves

1 Cook sweet potato in a medium saucepan of boiling water for 5 minutes or until tender. Drain well. Mash sweet potato; you will need 1 cup. Cool.

2 Bring the 2 cups water to a boil in a small saucepan. Stir in quinoa; cook, covered, over low heat for 15 minutes or until tender. Drain well. Cool.

3 Heat 1 tablespoon of the oil in a medium frying pan over medium heat; cook onion, stirring, for 8 minutes or until soft. Add garlic, ginger, chile, and curry powder; cook, stirring, over low heat for 3 minutes or until soft and fragrant.

4 Combine mashed sweet potato, quinoa, and onion mixture in a large bowl with cilantro, egg, and flour; season. Form level ½-cups of mixture into eight 3¼-inch patties. Place on a baking sheet lined with parchment paper. Cover; refrigerate for 30 minutes or until chilled.

5 Heat 1the remaining oil in a large frying pan over medium heat; cook patties, in batches, for 3 minutes each side or until golden and heated through. Drain on paper towel.

6 Heat 1 tablespoon oil in same frying pan over medium heat; cook tomatoes, mustard seeds, and curry leaves, stirring occasionally, for 5 minutes or until tomato is softened. Season to taste.

7 Serve quinoa cakes with tomatoes, yogurt, and salad leaves.

prep + cook time 50 minutes (+ cooling & refrigeration)
serves 4
nutritional count per serving 31.4g total fat (6.3g saturated fat); 611 cal; 61.5g carbohydrate; 16g protein; 8.9g fiber

This textural salad of grains, nuts, and fruits can be eaten as a light lunch, or serve it as a side dish with chicken or lamb. Grapes would make a nice alternative to the cherries.

chickpea, barley, orange, and cherry salad

You will need to soak the barley in cold water for 3 hours before you start this recipe. Drain barley before use.

1½ cups pearl barley

1 pound butternut squash, cut into ¾-inch pieces

1 tablespoon olive oil

2 teaspoons cumin seeds

2 medium oranges

12½ ounces canned chickpeas, drained, rinsed

⅓ cup almonds, roasted, chopped coarsely

¼ cup sunflower seeds, toasted lightly

½ pound cherries, halved, pitted

¼ cup chopped fresh mint, plus 2 tablespoons small fresh mint leaves, for garnish

2 tablespoons chopped fresh flat-leaf parsley

2 tablespoons pomegranate molasses

½ cup extra-virgin olive oil

1 Preheat oven to 425°F.

2 Cook soaked barley in a large saucepan of boiling water for 25 minutes or until tender; drain. Rinse under cold water; drain well.

3 Meanwhile, combine squash, olive oil, and cumin seeds on a large baking sheet; season. Bake for 20 minutes or until tender and beginning to brown around edges.

4 Remove zest from oranges with a zester, into long thin strips. Segment oranges over a bowl to catch the juices (see tip); reserve 2 tablespoons of juice.

5 Place barley, squash, orange segments, and zest in a large bowl with chickpeas, nuts, seeds, cherries, and herbs. Combine reserved juice, pomegranate molasses, and extra-virgin olive oil in a small jar. Drizzle dressing over salad, season to taste; toss gently to combine. Garnish salad with small mint leaves.

prep + cook time 45 minutes (+ standing) **serves** 4
nutritional count per serving 49.1g total fat (6.7g saturated fat); 904 cal; 87.3g carbohydrate; 19.1g protein; 22.5g fiber

tip To segment oranges: cut top and bottom from oranges with a small sharp knife. Cut remaining zest and white pith from oranges, following the curve of the fruit. Holding the oranges over a bowl, cut down both sides of the white membrane to release each segment. Squeeze membrane to release any juices into the bowl.

seeded pumpkin bread

1¾-pound butternut squash,
halved lengthwise, seeds removed

2 teaspoons dried yeast

1 tablespoon honey

½ cup lukewarm water

2 tablespoons vegetable oil

1⅓ cups whole-wheat flour

2 cups "00" flour, bread flour, or all-purpose flour

½ cup sunflower seeds

2 tablespoons sesame seeds

1 tablespoon flaxseeds

1 tablespoon sea salt flakes

1 egg, beaten lightly

2 tablespoons pepitas (pumpkin seeds)

2 teaspoons poppyseeds

1 Preheat oven to 350°F.

2 Place squash on a baking sheet, cover with foil; bake for 1¼ hours or until very tender. When cool enough to handle, scoop flesh into a medium bowl; mash with a fork. You will need 1½ cups mashed squash.

3 Combine yeast, honey, and the water in a small bowl; cover with plastic wrap. Stand in a warm place for 10 minutes or until frothy. Stir in oil.

4 Combine flours, seeds, and salt in a large bowl. Add yeast mixture and mashed squash; mix to a soft dough. Knead dough on a floured surface for 10 minutes or until smooth and elastic. (If you have an electric mixer with a dough hook, mix on medium speed for 6 minutes or until smooth and elastic.) Place dough in a large oiled bowl; cover with plastic wrap. Let stand in a warm place for 1 hour or until doubled in size.

5 Increase oven to 425°F. Punch down the dough with your fist. Knead on a floured surface 1 minute or until smooth. Shape dough into an 8-inch round; place on a large oiled baking sheet. Cover loosely with oiled plastic wrap. Stand in a warm place for 40 minutes or until almost doubled in size.

6 Brush dough with egg, sprinkle with pepitas and poppyseeds. Using a sharp, thin-bladed knife, make five shallow cuts across the top of the dough. Bake for 20 minutes. Reduce oven to 350°F; bake a further 10 minutes or until golden and bread sounds hollow when tapped. Cool on a wire rack.

prep + cook time 2 hours (+ standing) **serves** 8
nutritional count per serving 14.4g total fat (1.6g saturated fat); 411 cal; 53.5g carbohydrate; 12.3g protein; 8.7g fiber

Traditionally, harira is a Moroccan soup of lamb, vegetables, and pulses, popularly served to break the fast of Ramadan. Our version omits the meat.

vegetable harira soup

You will need to start this recipe the day before.

1 cup dried chickpeas (garbanzo beans)

large pinch saffron threads

4 pounds ripe tomatoes

2 tablespoons olive oil

2 medium onions, chopped coarsely

2 sticks celery, trimmed, chopped coarsely

1½ teaspoons ground cinnamon

1 teaspoon ground turmeric

1 teaspoon ground ginger

5 cups water

1 cup dried French-style green lentils

½ cup coarsely chopped fresh flat-leaf parsley

½ cup coarsely chopped fresh cilantro

1 Soak chickpeas overnight in a medium bowl of cold water. Drain; rinse well.

2 Soak saffron in a small bowl with 1 tablespoon water.

3 Cut a shallow cross in the base of tomatoes; place in a large bowl. Cover with boiling water, let stand for 30 seconds; drain. Remove skins and discard; puree flesh in a blender.

4 Heat oil in a large saucepan over medium heat; cook onion, celery, ground spices, and saffron with soaking liquid, stirring for 5 minutes or until vegetables have softened. Add pureed tomatoes, the water and chickpeas; bring to a boil. Skim off any scum that rises to the surface. Reduce heat to low; simmer, partially covered, for 45 minutes. Add lentils; simmer, partially covered, for 45 minutes or until lentils and chickpeas are tender. Season with salt.

5 Stir half the herbs through soup. Divide soup among bowls; serve topped with remaining herbs.

prep + cook time 2 hours (+ standing) **serves** 6
nutritional count per serving 14.1g total fat (2g saturated fat); 362 cal; 28.4g carbohydrate; 23.4g protein; 17.9g fiber

serving suggestion Serve with bread rolls.

Romesco is a traditional northern Spanish sauce, much like pesto in texture, made from a mixture of nuts and fire-roasted bell peppers that often accompanies seafood or a local roasted Catalonian spring onion.

romesco sauce with eggplant and zucchini

olive oil spray

2 medium eggplant, sliced on the diagonal

4 zucchini, sliced thinly, lengthwise

⅓ cup blanched almonds, roasted, chopped coarsely

⅓ cup skinless roasted hazelnuts, chopped coarsely

¼ cup fresh flat-leaf parsley leaves, torn

romesco sauce

2 medium red bell pepper

1 medium tomato

2 tablespoons extra-virgin olive oil

2 cloves garlic

2 teaspoons sweet paprika

½ cup blanched almonds, roasted

½ cup skinless roasted hazelnuts

2 tablespoons sherry or red wine vinegar

¼ cup water

1 Make Romesco Sauce.
2 Preheat a grill pan to high. Spray vegetables with olive oil; season with salt. Cook vegetables, in batches, for 4 minutes each side until tender and lightly charred.
3 Layer vegetables on a platter; top with nuts and parsley. Serve with romesco sauce.

romesco sauce Roast bell peppers and tomato directly over a gas flame on stove-top, turning until charred (or roast in a hot heavy-based frying pan or grill pan, turning, until charred). Wrap individually in foil. Peel away skins. Chop bell peppers and tomato; keep separated. Heat half the oil in a medium frying pan over medium heat; cook chopped bell pepper and garlic, stirring occasionally, for 3 minutes or until bell pepper is soft. Add chopped tomato and paprika; cook for 3 minutes or until tomato softens. Process nuts until finely chopped; add bell pepper mixture, sherry, and the water, process until smooth. Season to taste.

prep + cook time 35 minutes (+ cooling) **serves** 4
nutritional count per serving 19.4g total fat (0.9g saturated fat); 271 cal; 8.9g carbohydrate; 8.4g protein; 10g fiber

tips Romesco sauce is also delicious with grilled meats and fish. The sauce can be stored in an airtight container in the fridge for up to 1 week.

Brazil nuts are a rich source of the antioxidant mineral selenium. Just 2-3 nuts are all you need to meet your daily requirement.

WALNUTS

ARE A STANDOUT FOR PLANT OMEGA-3 FAT ALPHA-LINOLENIC ACID (ALA), WITH 30G OF NUTS PROVIDING 1.9G. ALA CANNOT BE MADE IN THE BODY AND MUST BE OBTAINED FROM OUR DIET. IT SEEMS TO PLAY A ROLE IN HEART HEALTH WITH HARVARD RESEARCHERS RECOMMENDING AN INTAKE OF 2–3G A DAY.

Pistachios

are different from other nuts in that they contain beta-carotene, which can be converted to vitamin A, and lutein. Both vitamin A and lutein are essential for good eye health.

Pecans have an impressively high antioxidant score compared to other nuts. They are especially high in one form of vitamin E called gamma-tocopherols, which help to protect LDL cholesterol from damage.

nuts

Nuts contain many different nutrients that may account for their beneficial effects on health. They contain low levels of saturated fats and are rich in a variety of unsaturated fats. Pecans, pistachios, almonds, cashews, and hazelnuts provide predominantly monounsaturated fat—similar to the type of fat in olive oil. Brazil nuts, walnuts, and pine nuts are rich in polyunsaturated fats. These fats are known to improve blood cholesterol profiles. Nuts also contain vitamin E, antioxidants, folate, arginine, and plant sterols, all of which contribute to heart health.

Cashews and pine

nuts top the nut charts for iron and zinc. Try consuming with a vitamin-C rich piece of fruit to optimize iron intake, especially if you are a vegetarian.

Almonds are head and shoulders above other nuts for vitamin E. A handful is pretty much all you need for your daily vitamin E quota.

With their rich fat content, nuts are relatively energy-dense foods. Once upon a time, before we knew any better, they were therefore restricted foods on any weight loss diet. Fortunately nuts are back on the menu for weight control, with research clearly showing a benefit. Nuts are fiber and protein rich, both factors that slow stomach emptying and have the effect of helping you to feel full and keep hunger pangs at bay.

Eating a healthy breakfast with a good mix of slow-release carbs and protein will help to keep your blood sugar levels in check for the rest of the day. You can skip the poached pear part of this recipe if you like and top with a mix of fresh or frozen berries instead.

muesli with poached pears and sheep's milk yogurt

⅓ cup almond butter

⅓ cup pure maple syrup

2 cups rolled oats

1 cup flaked coconut

½ cup flaked almonds

¼ cup pepitas (pumpkin seeds)

¼ cup sunflower seeds

¼ cup quinoa flakes

¼ cup rolled amaranth or rolled rye

2 tablespoons black or white chia seeds

1 cup dried sweetened cranberries

6 small pears

2 cups apple juice

2 cups water

1½ cups sheep's milk yogurt

1 Preheat oven to 325°F. Line a large roasting pan with parchment paper.

2 Stir almond butter and maple syrup in a small saucepan over low heat just until combined.

3 Combine oats, coconut, nuts, pepitas, seeds, quinoa, and amaranth in a large bowl. Pour syrup mixture over dry ingredients; working quickly, stir to coat ingredients.

4 Spread muesli, in an even layer, in pan. Bake for 15 minutes. Remove from oven; stir well. Bake a further 5 minutes or until oats are golden. Cool for 10 minutes; stir in chia seeds and cranberries.

5 Meanwhile, peel, halve, and core pears, leaving stalks intact. Place pears in a medium saucepan with juice and the water; bring to a boil. Reduce heat; cover pears with a round of parchment paper, simmer 8 minutes or until tender.

6 Serve muesli topped with yogurt and poached pears. If you like, drizzle with honey.

prep + cook time 45 minutes **serves** 6
nutritional count per serving 36.8g total fat (9g saturated fat); 684 cal; 61g carbohydrate; 19g protein; 16g fiber

tips Similarly to quinoa, amaranth is treated as a grain. You will be able to find the ingredients for this muesli either in the health food aisle at most supermarkets, or at health food stores. The muesli will keep in an airtight container for up to 1 month.

Freekeh is roasted green wheat that contains more nutrients than the mature version of the same grain. It has a delicious nutty taste and toothsome texture and is available from major supermarkets and health food stores.

spiced freekeh with cucumber and garlic minted yogurt

2 tablespoons olive oil

1 large onion, chopped finely

2 cloves garlic, crushed

2 medium carrots, diced

1 teaspoon ground allspice

1 teaspoon ground cilantro

½ teaspoon chile powder

2 teaspoons cumin seeds

1½ cups cracked greenwheat freekeh

1 bay leaf

2½ cups vegetable stock or water

2 small lebanese cucumbers

1 fresh long green chile, sliced thinly

½ cup fresh cilantro leaves

½ cup flaked almonds, roasted

garlic minted yogurt

1½ cups Greek-style yogurt

2 garlic cloves, crushed

¼ cup finely chopped fresh mint

1 Heat oil in a large saucepan over medium heat; cook onion, garlic, and carrots, stirring, for 3 minutes. Add spices and seeds; cook, stirring, for 2 minutes. Stir in freekeh to coat. Add bay leaf and stock; bring to a boil. Reduce heat to low; cook, covered, for 20 minutes or until most of the liquid is absorbed. Remove from heat; stand, covered, for 10 minutes.

2 Meanwhile, make Garlic Minted Yogurt.

3 Using a vegetable peeler, peel cucumbers lengthwise into long thin ribbons.

4 Serve freekeh mixture topped with yogurt and cucumber; top with combined chile, cilantro and nuts.

garlic minted yogurt Combine ingredients in a bowl; season to taste.

prep + cook time 45 minutes **serves** 6
nutritional count per serving 19.4g total fat (4.3g saturated fat); 450 cal; 52g carbohydrate; 14.9g protein; 12.9g fiber

tip You can use 1 teaspoon ground cinnamon instead of the allspice, if you like.

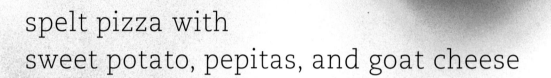

spelt pizza with
sweet potato, pepitas, and goat cheese

2 teaspoons active dry yeast

½ teaspoon salt

2 cups spelt flour

1 cup warm water

⅓ cup olive oil

3 medium onions, halved, sliced thinly

2 cloves garlic, crushed

1½ pounds orange sweet potatoes, sliced thinly

⅓ cup pepitas (pumpkin seeds)

1 fresh long green chile, seeded, chopped finely

7 ounces soft goat cheese, crumbled

¾ ounce baby arugula

1 Combine yeast, salt, and flour in a large bowl; make a well in the center. Stir in the water and 2 tablespoons of the oil until mixed well. Knead dough on a floured surface for 5 minutes until smooth and elastic. Place dough in an oiled bowl; cover with plastic wrap. Let stand for 30 minutes or until doubled in size.

2 Heat remaining oil in a large frying pan over medium-high heat; cook onion and garlic, stirring occasionally, for 5 minutes. Reduce heat to low; cook, stirring occasionally, for 20 minutes or until onion is light golden. Cool.

3 Preheat oven to 425°F. Oil two 12-inch pizza trays.

4 Divide dough in half, roll each half to a 10-inch round; place on tray. Spread onion mixture between pizza bases; top with sweet potatoes, slightly overlapping the slices, and pepitas.

5 Bake pizzas for 15 minutes, swapping trays halfway through cooking time, or until crust is golden. Serve topped with chile, cheese, and arugula.

prep + cook time 1 hour 20 minutes (+ standing) **serves** 4
nutritional count per serving 37.5g total fat (11g saturated fat); 840 cal; 91g carbohydrate; 29.4g protein; 18.5g fiber

tips Use a mandoline or V-slicer to easily cut the sweet potatoes into thin slices. For extra protein, add 2 tablespoons chia seeds to the pizza dough.

Raw bell peppers are often hard to digest. Long, slow cooking softens the texture and tempers the taste, accentuating their sweetness and making them easier to digest.

spelt pasta with braised bell peppers, nuts, and chile

¼ cup olive oil

1 medium onion, chopped finely

2 cloves garlic, crushed

1 teaspoon fennel seeds

3 medium red bell peppers, diced

3 medium yellow bell peppers, diced

1 fresh long red chile, seeded, chopped finely

2 tablespoons tomato paste

1¾ cups vegetable stock

2 tablespoons red wine vinegar

12 ounces spelt fettuccine

1 cup fresh basil leaves

2 tablespoons pine nuts, toasted

½ cup shaved parmesan

1 Heat oil in a large saucepan over medium-high heat; cook onion, garlic, and fennel seeds, stirring for 5 minutes. Add bell pepper and chile; cook, covered, stirring occasionally, for 8 minutes. Stir in tomato paste; cook for 2 minutes. Add stock; bring to a boil. Reduce heat; simmer, covered, for 25 minutes or until bell pepper is very tender. Remove from heat; stir in vinegar. Season to taste.
2 Meanwhile, cook pasta in a large saucepan of salted water until almost tender; drain. Return pasta to the pan.
3 Add bell pepper mixture to pasta with half the basil; toss to combine. Serve pasta in bowls topped with pine nuts, cheese, and remaining basil.

prep + cook time 50 minutes **serves** 4
nutritional count per serving 23.5g total fat (4.4g saturated fat); 648 cal; 81.4g carbohydrate; 24.6g protein; 9.5g fiber

Labne is yogurt that has been drained of whey. A short draining time results in a thick, creamy yogurt, while a longer one will achieve the consistency of a soft yogurt-cheese, which can be rolled into balls. You can make your own (see the recipe on page 32) or buy it from supermarkets.

mediterranean grain salad with honey cumin labne

¾ cup brown rice

½ cup dried French-style green lentils

½ cup red or white quinoa

1 cup water

1 small red onion, chopped finely

2 tablespoons pepitas (pumpkin seeds), toasted

2 tablespoons sunflower seeds, toasted

2 tablespoons pine nuts, toasted

2 tablespoons salted capers, rinsed

½ cup currants

1 cup firmly packed fresh flat-leaf parsley leaves

1 cup firmly packed fresh cilantro leaves

¼ cup lemon juice

⅓ cup olive oil

1 teaspoon cumin seeds, toasted

1 cup labne

1½ tablespoons honey

½ cup sliced almonds, roasted

1 Cook rice and lentils, separately, in large saucepans of boiling water for 25 minutes or until tender; drain, rinse well.
2 Place quinoa in a small saucepan with the water; bring to a boil. Reduce heat to low; simmer, covered, for 10 minutes or until tender. Drain.
3 Combine rice, lentils, and quinoa in a large bowl. Add onion, seeds, pine nuts, capers, currants, herbs, juic, and oil; stir until well combined.
4 Stir cumin seeds into labne in a small bowl.
5 Serve salad on plates or a large platter; top with spoonfuls of labne, drizzle with honey, and scatter with almonds.

prep + cook time 1 hour **serves** 6
nutritional count per serving 28.7g total fat (4.2g saturated fat); 555 cal; 56g carbohydrate; 15.5g protein; 8.2g fiber

tip Toast/roast all nuts and seeds together on a baking sheet (place the cumin seeds on a small piece of foil to keep them separate), in a 350°F oven for 8 minutes, stirring halfway through cooking time.

A recent

scientific review of 12 large-scale studies found a strong association between intake of whole grains and a 27–30% reduced risk of type 2 diabetes.

Whole grains do not deserve to be thrown into the same nutrition basket as products based on white flour. Big population studies from around the world have consistently shown that eating whole grains is good for us, reducing our risk of chronic diseases including heart disease, diabetes, stroke, and certain cancers, and helping us to live longer.

Where we can certainly go wrong is the form in which we eat our grains. Whole grains contain all three parts of the grain kernel — the bran, germ and endosperm, whereas the process used to make white flour removes the outer layers and only the starchy center, the endosperm, is used. Unfortunately this process removes a large percentage of the grain nutrients and phytochemicals along with the fiber. The end result is a refined starch product that inevitably has a high GI.

grains

Grains are staple foods of a majority of diverse cultures around the world, and have been for about 10,000 years. But in today's era of "carbophobia" grains are often unfairly labelled as "carbs" and considered fattening. You might be surprised to learn that the group comprising breads and cereals was the second most important source of protein in the daily diet in a major nutrition survey. They were also the largest source of fiber, thiamin, magnesium, and iron.

FREEKEH (PRONOUNCED FREE-KA) IS AN ANCIENT EASTERN MEDITERRANEAN GRAIN FOOD, MADE FROM ROASTED GREEN WHEAT. BECAUSE THE GRAIN IS HARVESTED WHILE YOUNG, IT HAS A FAR HIGHER NUTRIENT CONTENT, INCLUDING MORE PROTEIN, THAN MATURE WHEAT. IT HAS FOUR TIMES THE FIBER CONTENT OF BROWN RICE AND A LARGE PROPORTION OF THE CARBOHYDRATE PRESENT IS RESISTANT STARCH. THIS MEANS WE CAN'T BREAK IT DOWN AND IT ACTS LIKE A FIBER, PASSING THROUGH THE GUT TO THE COLON WHERE IT PROMOTES THE GROWTH OF FRIENDLY BACTERIA.

Diversify your intake of whole grains. Choose from barley, brown rice, freekeh, oats, rye, or the ancient grains spelt and kamut.

Freekeh is low GI, making it ideal for controlling blood glucose levels and weight control, and it's a good source of several nutrients, including iron, magnesium, thiamin, copper, and zinc.

We've left the skin on the pears in this recipe, as it has been shown to have twice the fiber of the flesh and a greater concentration of phytonutrients. Any bitterness from the skin and pepperiness from the watercress is easily balanced by the sweetness of the pear flesh.

pasta with almond and walnut paste, pears, and fava beans

½ cup almonds, roasted

½ cup walnuts, roasted

2 cloves garlic, crushed

1¾ cup firmly packed watercress sprigs

½ teaspoon freshly ground black pepper

½ cup extra-virgin olive oil

12½ ounces spelt penne pasta

2 medium pears, unpeeled, cored, cut into eight wedges

1 tablespoon olive oil

2 cups frozen fava beans, blanched, peeled

⅓ cup shaved pecorino or parmesan

1 Process nuts, garlic, ¼ cup watercress, and pepper until finely chopped. With motor operating, gradually pour in ¼ cup of the extra-virgin olive oil until combined. Season with salt to taste.

2 Cook pasta in a large saucepan of boiling salted water for 8 minutes or until almost tender. Drain; reserve ½ cup pasta cooking water. Return pasta to pan; cover to keep warm.

3 Meanwhile, season pears. Heat olive oil in a large frying pan over medium heat; cook pears for 2 minutes each side or until golden. Drain on paper towel.

4 Add nut paste to pasta with enough reserved cooking water for paste to coat pasta (do not return the pan to the heat or the nut paste will thicken and make the mixture dry). Add pear, beans, and remaining watercress; toss gently to combine. Season to taste.

5 Serve pasta topped with cheese, drizzled with remaining extra-virgin olive oil.

prep + cook time 25 minutes serves 4
nutritional count per serving 55.7g total fat (7.7g saturated fat); 999 cal; 89.9g carbohydrate; 28.5g protein; 14.2g fiber

tip The nut paste can be made a day ahead; store in an airtight container in the fridge until ready to use.

versatile veggies

Veggies contain a wealth of nutrients and phytochemicals that are essential for optimal health and well-being.

Kale is finally in the spotlight. And so it should be: it's a powerhouse of vitamins; tops milk for calcium; and has more iron than meat. Kale has myriad uses cooked or raw.

kale salad with creamy zucchini dressing

1 cup red or white quinoa

2 cups water

6½ ounces purple kale, trimmed, washed, shredded finely

1 large carrot, unpeeled, grated coarsely

1 cup walnuts, roasted, chopped coarsely

creamy zucchini dressing

2 small zucchini, chopped coarsely

1 large avocado, chopped coarsely

⅓ cup walnuts, roasted

1 clove garlic, crushed

2 tablespoons white wine vinegar

2 tablespoons walnut oil

2 tablespoons olive oil

1 Make Creamy Zucchini Dressing.
2 Place quinoa and the water in a medium saucepan; bring to a boil. Reduce heat to low; simmer, covered, for 10 minutes or until tender. Drain; cool.
3 Place quinoa in a large bowl with kale, carrot, nuts, and dressing; toss gently to combine. Season to taste.
creamy zucchini dressing Process zucchini, avocado, nuts, garlic, and vinegar until smooth. With motor operating, gradually add oils, drop by drop, then in a slow steady stream, until thick and creamy. Season to taste.

prep + cook time 25 minutes **serves** 6
nutritional count per serving 37.8g total fat (4.6g saturated fat); 487 cal; 24.8g carbohydrate; 9.4g protein; 6.6g fiber

tip Quinoa and walnuts are packed with ample protein to make this a meal in itself; however, you could serve it as a side dish with grilled chicken, fish, or a poached egg. It would also make a delicious filling for wraps or a sandwich.

serving suggestion Serve with grilled chicken breast fillet and lemon wedges.

Pleating the edge of the dumplings can be a little tricky. You can simply press the edges together to ensure they are well sealed—they will be just as tasty.

spinach and ginger dumplings

½ pound spinach

7 ounces canned water chestnuts, drained, chopped finely

2 green onions (scallions), chopped finely

1½-inch piece fresh ginger, grated finely

1 tablespoon light soy sauce

1 egg, beaten lightly

24 gow gee wrappers

14½ ounces firm tofu, sliced thickly

2 tablespoons vegetable oil

2 teaspoons sesame seeds, toasted

½ cup loosely packed fresh cilantro leaves

spicy dressing

½ cup Chinese black vinegar

1 tablespoon lemon juice

1 teaspoon sesame oil

1 fresh small red chile, sliced thinly

1 Make Spicy Dressing.
2 Place spinach in a medium heatproof bowl, cover with boiling water; drain immediately. Refresh under cold running water; drain. When cool enough to handle, squeeze excess water from spinach; chop finely.
3 Combine spinach, water chestnuts, onion, ginger, sauce, and egg in a bowl. Place 2 teaspoons of the mixture in the center of a wrapper, leaving a border; brush the edge with water. Fold wrapper over filling; pleat the edge to seal. Repeat with remaining spinach mixture and wrappers.
4 Cook dumplings in a large saucepan of boiling water, in three batches, for 3 minutes or until cooked through. Drain; keep warm.
5 Meanwhile, pat tofu dry with paper towel. Heat oil in a large frying pan over high heat; cook tofu for 2 minutes each side or until golden.
6 Divide tofu and dumplings among bowls; drizzle with dressing, then sprinkle with sesame seeds and cilantro.
spicy dressing Combine ingredients in a small bowl.

prep + cook time 30 minutes **serves** 4
nutritional count per serving 23.8g total fat (4g saturated fat); 463 cal; 34g carbohydrate; 21.2g protein; 12g fiber

tip Chinese black vinegar is made from fermented glutinous rice, is mildly acidic and slightly sweet, and is used as a condiment. It is available from Asian food stores (the Chinkiang brand is one of the best). You can use rice vinegar instead.

Superfood greens include spinach, chard, kale, cabbage varieties, endive, watercress, and Asian greens.

Two of the world's healthiest diets, the Mediterranean diet and the Okinawan diet, have a few common features—one of those is their inclusion of leafy greens.

KALE IS ONE OF THE MOST NUTRITIOUS VEGGIES. IT'S PARTICULARLY RICH IN CAROTENOIDS THAT CAN BE CONVERTED TO VITAMIN A IN THE BODY. A SINGLE CUP OF KALE PROVIDES YOU WITH OVER 200% OF YOUR DAILY RECOMMENDED AMOUNT OF VITAMIN A. KALE IS ONE OF THE BEST SOURCES OF THE CAROTENOIDS LUTEIN AND ZEAXANTHIN. THESE ARE KNOWN TO PLAY AN ESSENTIAL ROLE IN EYE HEALTH. A HIGH DIETARY INTAKE IS ASSOCIATED WITH A REDUCED RISK OF AGE-RELATED MACULAR DEGENERATION AND CATARACTS. KALE IS ALSO TERRIFIC FOR VITAMIN C, VITAMIN K, VITAMIN B6, CALCIUM, POTASSIUM, COPPER, AND MANGANESE, AND SUPPLIES GOOD LEVELS OF SEVERAL B-GROUP VITAMINS INCLUDING FOLATE, IRON, MAGNESIUM, AND PHOSPHORUS.

leafy greens

Leafy greens are without doubt one of the top superfoods for you to include in your daily diet. They are among the most nutrient-dense foods, yet contain very few calories and they're anti-inflammatory. That's great news for those of us watching our weight—and that's just about every one of us.

Spinach is one of the most versatile leafy greens and therefore super easy to use to nutrient-boost your day. It contains many of the nutrients found in kale, although in lower amounts for most, but is a better source of folate. Folate is well known for its benefits during early pregnancy, but in fact we all need a decent daily folate hit due to its role in protecting cells and DNA from damage. A high folate intake can slow the aging process and reduce the risk of many chronic diseases. A cup of spinach gives you about 15% of your recommended intake of folate and over half your vitamin A, all for only 7 calories.

Bulk up your meal with leafy greens and you achieve volume to help fill you up without the extra calories, truckloads of nutrients and plant chemicals that benefit your health, and boost your fiber intake to help keep your gut healthy. There are plenty to choose from, and generally the darker the leaves the better, but aim for variety. Freshness is key as many nutrients, including vitamin C, will deteriorate with time and exposure to air and light.

Leaving fruit and vegetables unpeeled not only speeds up preparation time, it also makes good nutritional sense, upping the fiber content of a dish (and in the case of sweet potatoes, the antioxidant content), since the skin contains triple that of the flesh.

roast sweet potato and pear salad with crunchy chickpeas

12½ ounces canned chickpeas, drained, rinsed

¼ cup olive oil

1 tablespoon fennel seeds

2 tablespoons chopped fresh rosemary leaves

1¼ pounds small orange sweet potatoes, unpeeled, cut into wedges

2 medium pears, unpeeled, cut into eight wedges

¼ cup dried sweetened cranberries

1 cup boiling water

1 cup Greek-style yogurt

1 tablespoon tahini

6½ ounces arugula

1 Preheat oven to 425°F.

2 Pat chickpeas dry with paper towels; place on a baking sheet. Drizzle 1 tablespoon of the oil over chickpeas, sprinkle with half the fennel seeds and half the rosemary; season. Bake for 20 minutes, stirring occasionally, or until chickpeas are golden and crisp.

3 Reduce oven to 350°F. Combine sweet potato and pears on a large baking sheet with remaining oil, fennel, and rosemary; season. Bake for 40 minutes or until sweet potato and pears are browned and tender.

4 Meanwhile, soak cranberries in a boiling water for 10 minutes or until softened. Drain, reserving 2 tablespoons of the soaking liquid.

5 Combine yogurt, tahini, and reserved cranberry soaking liquid in a small bowl; season to taste.

6 To serve, arrange arugula, sweet potato, and pears on a large platter; top with chickpeas and cranberries, then drizzle with yogurt mixture.

prep + cook time 1 hour 15 minutes **serves** 4
nutritional count per serving 23.4g total fat (5.4g saturated fat); 571 cal; 66.1g carbohydrate; 14.6g protein; 13.9g fiber

japanese-style vegetable, tofu, and noodle broth

8 dried shiitake mushrooms

1 cup boiling water

12½ ounces small choy sum

6½ ounces soba noodles

1 tablespoon peanut oil

4 green onions (scallions), sliced thinly

1½-inch piece fresh ginger, chopped finely

6 cups vegetable stock

¼ cup soy sauce

1 teaspoon sesame oil

5½ ounces asparagus, chopped

6½ ounces snow peas, chopped

⅔ cup frozen shelled edamame, thawed

9½ ounce silken tofu, cut into 12 pieces

1 cup pea tendrils, trimmed

1 Soak mushrooms in a boiling water in a small heatproof bowl for 20 minutes. Drain; reserving soaking liquid. Remove and discard mushroom stems; slice caps.
2 Meanwhile, cut stalks from choy sum. Cut stalks into 4-inch lengths; cut leaves into 4-inch pieces. Keep stalks and leaves separated.
3 Cook noodles in a large saucepan of boiling water 4 minutes or until just tender. Drain; rinse under cold water, drain well.
4 Heat peanut oil in a large saucepan over medium heat; cook onion and ginger, stirring, for 3 minutes or until soft. Add mushrooms, reserved soaking liquid and stock; bring to a boil. Reduce heat; simmer for 10 minutes.
5 Add sauce, sesame oil, asparagus, snow peas, and choy sum stalks; simmer for 2 minutes or until almost tender. Add choy sum leaves and edamame; simmer for 1 minute or until vegetables are tender. Season to taste.
6 Divide noodles and tofu among bowls. Spoon vegetables and broth on top; top with pea tendrils.

prep + cook time 45 minutes **serves** 4
nutritional count per serving 11.8g total fat (2g saturated fat); 329 cal; 26.6g carbohydrate; 25g protein; 12g fiber

tip Pea tendrils are the tendrils from the vines of a pea plant; they have a mild pea taste and are used in salads and stir-fries. They are available from Asian grocers and specialty grocers. You can use snow pea shoots instead.

Herbs such as basil, mint, and cilantro add more than just freshness to our plates. Their leaves are rich in flavonoids and are surprisingly high sources of vitamins A and C. Cilantro is one of the richest herbal sources of vitamin K.

coconut-roasted pumpkin and cauliflower with chile, lime, and cashews

1 small kabocha squash (2 pounds), unpeeled, cut into thick wedges

½ large cauliflower, cut into large florets

2 tablespoons coconut oil, melted

⅓ cup shaved coconut, roasted

⅓ cup raw cashews, roasted

¼ cup fresh cilantro leaves

¼ cup fresh mint leaves

¼ cup fresh thai basil leaves

dressing

2 teaspoons lime juice

2 tablespoons fish sauce

2 tablespoons brown sugar

2 tablespoons peanut oil

1 fresh long red chile, chopped finely

2 tablespoons chopped fresh cilantro

1 Preheat oven to 425°F.
2 Place squash and cauliflower on a large baking sheet; brush with coconut oil, season. Bake for 30 minutes or until vegetables are brown and tender.
3 Meanwhile, make dressing.
4 To serve, arrange squash and cauliflower on a large platter; drizzle with dressing. Sprinkle with coconut, nuts, and herbs.
dressing Combine ingredients in a small jar.

prep + cook time 50 minutes **serves** 4
nutritional count per serving 27.7g total fat (13.2g saturated fat); 420 cal; 28.7g carbohydrate; 9.5g protein; 11.3g fiber

tips Coconut oil is a solidified oil sold in jars and is available from major supermarkets and health food stores. Melt coconut oil as you would butter, either in a small saucepan over low heat or in the microwave. You will need 2 limes for this recipe.

BETA-CAROTENE CAN BE CONVERTED TO VITAMIN A IN THE BODY AND THIS IS IMPORTANT SINCE VITAMIN A IS NOT SO WIDELY DISTRIBUTED IN FOODS. AN EXCESS OF VITAMIN A CAN ALSO BE TOXIC (IT IS PARTICULARLY HARMFUL DURING PREGNANCY), WHILE THERE IS NO DANGER OF THIS FROM AMPLE BETA-CAROTENE-RICH FOODS. A WORD OF WARNING, HOWEVER—SUPPLEMENTS ARE NOT THE SAME. WHILE BETA-CAROTENE RICH DIETS HAVE BEEN SHOWN TO BENEFIT HEALTH, SUPPLEMENTS DO NOT HAVE THE SAME EFFECT AND CAN BE HARMFUL. STICK TO REAL FOODS TO GAIN ALL THE BENEFITS WITHOUT ANY RISKS.

BETA-CAROTENE is what makes carrots (where beta-carotene got its name), sweet potato, and pumpkin orange. Many orange colored fruits, including pawpaw and apricots, are also sources of beta-carotene. You'll also find high levels of carotenoids in leafy greens such as kale, spinach, and cabbage. In these foods the green color of chlorophyll masks the orange carotenoids, but they are there in abundance.

carotenoid veggies

You have no doubt heard of the most famous carotenoid, beta-carotene, but in fact there are a whole family of related plant carotenoid compounds, all with their own benefits. Some act as antioxidants, some can be converted to vitamin A in the body, and others have specifically been associated with reduced risk of disease.

LYCOPENE is the carotenoid found in tomatoes, but also in red grapefruit, goji berries, guava, and papaya. High intakes of lycopene have been associated with a reduced risk of cancer, particularly prostate cancer in men. The amazing thing about lycopene is that it is better absorbed from processed tomatoes than fresh. Tomato paste is a pretty unbeatable source, particularly when teamed with extra-virgin olive oil in an Italian-style dish. Carotenoids are fat soluble and so a little healthy fat in the recipe boosts your absorption.

LUTEIN & ZEAXANTHIN Two other carotenoids deserve mention—lutein and zeaxanthin. They are found in high concentrations in the eye and seem to play a crucial role in eye development and ongoing eye health throughout life. Those with diets high in these two carotenoids reduce the risk of macular degeneration and cataracts. You'll find them in those dark leafy greens such as kale, spinach, and broccoli, as well as in egg yolks.

Broccoli, brussels sprouts, and kale are all crucifers—members of the cabbage family, known for its sulphur content, which is dectectable when these vegetables are overcooked. Sulforaphane, though, is a powerful phytochemical that may protect against cancer.

winter vegetable sauté with prosciutto and hazelnuts

½ pound broccoli, cut into florets

½ pound baby brussels sprouts

10 ounces purple curly kale, trimmed, chopped coarsely

1 medium lemon

2 tablespoons olive oil

4½ ounces whole-grain sourdough bread, cut into pieces

2½ ounces thinly sliced prosciutto, chopped

1 large onion, sliced thinly

4 cloves garlic, sliced thinly

⅓ cup hazelnuts, roasted, chopped coarsely

½ cup chicken stock

1 Cook broccoli in a large saucepan of boiling water for 2 minutes or until just tender but still crisp. Drain immediately; refresh in iced water. Drain well. Repeat with sprouts, then kale.
2 Remove zest from lemon with a zester, into long thin strips (or grate finely). Squeeze juice from lemon; you will need 2 tablespoons juice.
3 Heat half the oil in a large frying pan over medium heat; cook bread pieces, stirring, for 5 minutes or until golden. Remove from pan.
4 Heat remaining oil in same pan over medium heat; cook prosciutto, stirring, for 2 minutes or until crisp. Remove with a slotted spoon; drain on paper towel. Reduce heat to medium-low; cook onion, stirring, for 10 minutes or until very soft. Add garlic; stir for 2 minutes. Add vegetables, zest, and nuts; cook, stirring for 5 minutes until combined.
5 Increase heat to high, add stock and juice; simmer 1 minute or until vegetables are tender. Season to taste. Just before serving, scatter with toasted bread.

prep + cook time 45 minutes **serves** 4
nutritional count per serving 20.6g total fat (3g saturated fat); 363 cal; 21.5g carbohydrate; 17.4g protein; 11.3g fiber

While walnuts and other tree nuts are fairly calorific, they offer a veritable array of antioxidant and anti-inflammatory nutrients, as well as valuable monounsaturated and hard-to-source omega-3 fatty acids. If you like, you can use almonds instead of walnuts in the pesto.

spinach and broccolini pasta with arugula and walnut pesto

¾ pound whole-wheat spaghetti

15 ounces broccolini, trimmed, cut into 1½-inch lengths

2 tablespoons olive oil

2 cloves garlic, crushed

¾ pound baby spinach

1 cup ricotta, crumbled

½ cup walnuts, roasted, chopped coarsely

arugula and walnut pesto

2 ounces arugula leaves

1 cup firmly packed fresh basil leaves

½ cup walnuts, roasted

2 cloves garlic, crushed

1 teaspoon finely grated lemon zest

⅓ cup finely grated parmesan

½ cup extra-virgin olive oil

1 Make Arugula and Walnut Pesto.
2 Cook pasta in a large saucepan of boiling salted water for 10 minutes or until almost tender, adding broccolini in last 2 minutes of cooking. Drain well; reserve ½ cup cooking water.
3 Meanwhile, heat oil in a large saucepan over medium heat; cook garlic and spinach, stirring occasionally, for 2 minutes or until just wilted. Season. Add pasta, broccolini, pesto, and enough reserved cooking water to help combine the sauce.
4 Serve pasta topped with ricotta and nuts.

arugula and walnut pesto Process arugula, basil, nuts, garlic, zest, cheese, and 1 tablespoon of the oil until roughly chopped. With motor operating, add remaining oil in a thin, steady stream until mixture is smooth. Season to taste.

prep + cook time 35 minutes **serves** 6
nutritional count per serving 42.4g total fat (7.8g saturated fat); 674 cal; 49.5g carbohydrate; 20.7g protein; 6.8g fiber

tip It's a good idea to remove the thin paper skins from the walnuts after roasting, as they can add a slight bitterness to the pesto. While the nuts are still warm, rub them together in a clean tea towel to remove most of the skins.

napa cabbage and herb salad
with beef and tamarind dressing

1 tablespoon vegetable oil

½ pound beef stir-fry strips

½ small napa cabbage, shredded finely

1 fresh long red chile, sliced thinly

¾ cup roasted peanuts, chopped coarsely

3 ounces baby spinach leaves

1½ cups fresh mint leaves

½ cup loosely packed fresh Vietnamese mint leaves

tamarind dressing

1½ tablespoons tamarind puree

½ cup brown rice syrup

2 tablespoons lime juice

2 tablespoons fish sauce

1 Make Tamarind Dressing.

2 Heat oil in a wok over high heat; stir-fry beef for 3 minutes or until cooked through.

3 Place beef in a large bowl with napa cabbage, chile, peanuts, spinach, herbs, and dressing; toss gently to combine.

tamarind dressing Whisk ingredients in a bowl until combined.

prep + cook time 15 minutes **serves** 4
nutritional count per serving 19g total fat (2.6g saturated fat); 455 cal; 41.3g carbohydrate; 28.3g protein; 7g fiber

tips Brown rice syrup is also known as rice syrup or rice malt. It is available in the health food section in most supermarkets. Use prawns, chicken, or tofu instead of the beef.

Chard is high in non-heme iron, which is important in a vegetarian diet. Iron from plant sources isn't absorbed as well as heme iron from meat. Including vitamin C either in the dish (we used lemon juice in this recipe) or with the meal can aid absorption.

chard risotto

This recipe is based on the classic Greek leek and rice dish called prasorizo.

8 cups water

1½ pounds swiss chard

2 tablespoons olive oil

2 medium leeks, white part only, sliced thinly

2 cloves garlic, crushed

1 cup long-grain or medium-grain brown rice

¼ cup lemon juice

⅓ cup finely chopped fresh dill

¼ cup finely chopped fresh flat-leaf parsley

⅓ cup pine nuts, toasted

1½ tablespoons extra-virgin olive oil

⅓ cup feta, crumbled

1 tablespoon finely grated lemon zest

1 medium lemon, cut into wedges

1 Bring the water to a boil in a large saucepan. Reduce heat; keep at a gentle simmer.

2 Cut chard stalks from leaves. Trim ¾ inch off the end of the stalks; cut stalks into thick slices. Shred chard leaves. Keep stalks and leaves separated.

3 Heat olive oil in a large, deep frying pan over medium-high heat; cook chard stalks, leeks, and garlic, stirring occasionally, for 2 minutes or until just softened. Season. Add rice; cook, stirring, for 1 minute until coated.

4 Stir in 1 cup of the simmering water; cook, stirring over medium-low heat or until liquid is absorbed. Continue adding water, 1 cup at a time, stirring frequently or until water is absorbed after each addition. (You may not need all the liquid if you're using long-grain rice.) Total cooking time should be 45 minutes, or until rice is almost al dente. Stir in shredded chard leaves; cook a further 5 minutes or until leaves wilt.

5 Remove pan from heat. Stir in juice, herbs, and half the pine nuts; season to taste. Spoon mixture into bowls; drizzle with extra-virgin olive oil, top with feta, zest, and remaining pine nuts. Serve with lemon wedges.

prep + cook time 1 hour **serves** 4
nutritional count per serving 30.4g total fat (5.8g saturated fat); 531 cal; 45.7g carbohydrate; 13.6g protein; 10.5g fiber

tip You will need about 1 bunch of chard for this recipe.

Sichuan is a province in southwest China known for its abundant use of chile and eye-wateringly fiery dishes. For a milder dish, simply halve the Sichuan peppercorns, chiles, and chile flakes in the recipe below.

sichuan gai lan

1 pound broccolini

4 green onions (scallions), white and green parts

2 teaspoons Sichuan peppercorns

¼ cup grape seed oil

1 tablespoon brown rice syrup

4 fresh long red chiles, chopped coarsely

2 teaspoons dried chile flakes

4 cloves garlic, crushed

¾ pound gai lan, cut into thirds

¼ pound green beans, trimmed

½ cup water

6½ ounces marinated tofu, sliced

2 tablespoons light soy sauce

1 Cut broccolini in half; keep stems and tops separated. Coarsely chop the white part of the onion; thinly slice the green part. Keep white and green parts separated.
2 Dry-fry peppercorns in a wok over medium heat, stirring continuously, for 2 minutes or until fragrant. Gzest peppercorns in a small food processor. Add oil, rice syrup, chile, chile flakes, garlic, and white part of onion; process until finely chopped.
3 Cook chile mixture in wok over medium-high heat, stirring, for 3 minutes or until fragrant. Add broccolini stems, gai lan, beans, and the water; stir-fry for 1 minute. Add broccolini tops, tofu, and sauce; stir-fry for 2 minutes or until tofu is heated through and vegetables are just tender. Serve sprinkled with green part of onion.

prep + cook time 15 minutes **serves** 4
nutritional count per serving 18g total fat (2.7g saturated fat); 284 cal; 9g carbohydrate; 15.6g protein; 13g fiber

tips You will need 2 bunches of broccolini for this recipe. Substitute any of the vegetables in this recipe with another Asian green. Tofu can be substituted with barbecued chicken or smoked chicken breast.

Avocado

As well as providing a rich source of healthy monounsaturated fats, avocado is an impressively good source of fiber. Half an avocado contains 6–7g of fiber—almost a quarter of your daily goal. You may also be surprised to know that avocados are a good source of vitamin C. This makes them a great addition to a vegetarian meal as they will help you to absorb more plant iron.

Half an avocado also provides about a fifth of your daily folate needs. Folate protects your DNA and cells all around the body from damage and therefore plays a key role in anti-aging.

OLIVE OIL

THE MEDITERRANEAN DIET IS HAILED QUITE RIGHTFULLY AS ONE OF THE HEALTHIEST IN THE WORLD. THIS DIET HAS BEEN ASSOCIATED WITH LOWER RATES OF HEART DISEASE, LOWER BLOOD PRESSURE, LOWER RISK OF STROKE, BETTER COGNITIVE HEALTH, LOWER RISK OF DIABETES, AND LOWER RISKS OF MANY CANCERS. THERE ARE MANY FACTORS THAT MAY CONTRIBUTE TO THIS, BUT ONE OF THE KEY CHARACTERISTICS IS THE USE OF OLIVE OIL AS A STAPLE FOOD AND THE PRINCIPAL FAT.

avocado & oil

Remember when we tried to avoid fat of any kind? We now know that eating the right fats is essential for optimal health. Both avocado and olive oil are rich in monounsaturated fats and the only fruits that are fat rich. A solid body of scientific evidence supports making these fats the major ones in your diet. They can help you to achieve a healthier blood cholesterol profile, improve your insulin sensitivity, help you to control blood glucose levels, improve a fatty liver, and even reduce the amount of fat you store around your abdomen. What great news!

It is important to buy extra-virgin olive oil, however, and not products labeled as "light," "pure olive oil," or "pomace." These are all refined products and do not contain the health-promoting qualities of fresh extra-virgin olive oil. Refining the oil removes many of the antioxidants, phytosterols, and polyphenols present in the fresh extra-virgin oil that benefit us. Oil is not like wine—it doesn't get better with age. The fresher it is, the better. Choose quality over quantity and you will reap the benefits.

It's a myth that cooking with extra-virgin olive oil destroys its benefits. Good quality extra-virgin olive oil has a high smoke point of around 375 degrees. It can be used for stir-fries, on the BBQ, roasting foods in the oven, and pan-frying. Store your oil in a cool, dark place to retain the freshness and health-promoting properties. And use it regularly so that you are always consuming this year's batch.

Traditional larb is a tangy salad of minced pork (or chicken) and fresh herbs, originating from Laos, but also found in northern Thailand. This version keeps the traditional flavors and instead mixes them with the crisp textures of raw vegetables.

vegetable larb

2 tablespoons fish sauce

2 tablespoons lime juice

½ teaspoon dried chile flakes

1 medium beet, peeled, cut into ¼-inch pieces

1 large carrot unpeeled, cut into ¼-inch pieces

5 ounces yardlong beans, cut into ¼-inch pieces

1 large Persian cucumber, halved lengthwise

¼ cup jasmine rice

6½ ounces small cherry tomatoes, halved

3 green onions (scallions), sliced thinly

½ cup finely chopped fresh mint

2 tablespoons finely chopped fresh Thai basil or cilantro

⅓ cup roasted unsalted peanuts, chopped finely

1 head butter (Boston) lettuce, leaves separated

1 Preheat oven to 350°F.

2 Combine fish sauce, juice, and chile flakes in a large bowl.

3 Combine beet and 1 tablespoon of the dressing in a small bowl. Combine carrot, beans, and 2 tablespoons of the dressing in a medium bowl. Remove seeds from cucumber; cut into ¼-inch pieces. Add cucumber to remaining dressing in large bowl. Cover each bowl with plastic wrap; let stand for 15 minutes.

4 Meanwhile, place rice on a baking sheet; roast for 12 minutes or until golden. Process rice in a small food processor (or crush with a mortar and pestle) until very finely chopped.

5 Add tomatoes to cucumber mixture with onion, herbs, ground rice, carrot mixture, and half the nuts. Strain beet mixture through a sieve, add to larb; toss gently to combine.

6 Serve larb with lettuce leaves, sprinkled with remaining nuts.

prep + cook time 30 minutes **serves** 4 as a side dish
nutritional count per serving 5.8g total fat (0.8g saturated fat); 187 cal; 21.2g carbohydrate; 7.8g protein; 8.1g fiber

tip You will need about half a small bunch of yardlong beans for this recipe.

This zippy lasagne packs in the flavor with plenty of green vegetables, layered with a tangy but healthy béchamel and whole-wheat pasta.

pea, fennel, and spinach lasagne

6 tablespoons extra-virgin olive oil

1 medium bulb fennel, chopped finely

2 cloves garlic, crushed

2 shallots, chopped finely

1 teaspoon ground fennel

2 teaspoons finely grated lemon zest

1 pound spinach, trimmed

1½ cups fresh peas

2½ pounds canned chopped tomatoes

1 cup roughly torn fresh basil leaves, plus ¼ cup small basil leaves

8 ounces whole-wheat lasagne sheets

¼ cup soft ricotta

ricotta béchamel

1¾ cups soft ricotta

3 eggs

½ cup Greek-style yogurt

¼ cup lemon juice

1 cup crumbled feta

½ cup sparkling mineral water

1 Heat 1½ tablespoons of the oil in a large frying pan over medium heat; cook fennel, garlic, shallots, and ground fennel, stirring, for 8 minutes or until lightly golden. Transfer mixture to a large bowl; stir in zest. Season to taste.

2 Wash spinach leaves but don't dry. Cook spinach in same pan over high heat, in two batches, until wilted; drain. When cool enough to handle, squeeze out excess liquid. Coarsely chop spinach; stir into fennel mixture. Season to taste. Refrigerate until cooled. Stir in peas.

3 Preheat oven to 400°F.

4 Combine tomatoes, basil, and 2½ tablespoons oil in a bowl; season.

5 Make Ricotta Béchamel.

6 Spread one-third of the tomato mixture over the base of a 3-quart baking dish. Cover with one-third of the pasta sheets. Top with half the spinach mixture and half the ricotta béchamel. Continue layering with remaining pasta sheets, tomato mixture, spinach mixture, and ricotta béchamel; finishing with pasta sheets and tomato mixture. Top with spoonfuls of ricotta.

7 Bake lasagne for 45 minutes or until top is golden and pasta is cooked (cover with greased foil if necessary to prevent overbrowning). Let stand for 10 minutes before serving. Serve lasagne drizzled with 2 tablespoons oil and topped with small basil leaves.

ricotta béchamel Whisk ricotta, eggs, yogurt, juice, and feta in a large bowl until combined. Whisk mineral water into mixture until combined.

prep + cook time 1 hour 10 minutes (+ cooling) **serves** 6
nutritional count per serving 35g total fat (13.5g saturated fat); 630 cal; 43.6g carbohydrate; 29.3g protein; 11.8g fiber

Water spinach is a delicious Asian green with small elongated leaves and succulent hollow stems. Both the mild-tasting stems and leaves are eaten.

stir-fried pumpkin, water spinach, and tomatoes with five spice

¼ cup extra-virgin coconut oil, melted

1¼ pounds kabocha squash, peeled, cut into 1¼-inch pieces

2 teaspoons Chinese five-spice powder

¼ cup oyster sauce

¼ cup water

2½-inch piece fresh ginger, cut into fine matchsticks

6 ounces water spinach, trimmed, cut into thirds

½ pound cherry tomatoes, halved

⅓ cup sliced almonds, roasted

1 Heat 2 tablespoons of the coconut oil in a large wok over medium heat; cook squash pieces, turning frequently, for 6 minutes until almost tender. Remove from wok.
2 Meanwhile, combine five-spice, oyster sauce, and the water in a small bowl.
3 Heat remaining oil in wok over medium-high heat; stir-fry ginger for 1 minute or until crisp. Add water spinach, tomatoes, and five-spice mixture; stir-fry for 1 minute or until water spinach wilts. Return squash to wok; stir through.
4 Serve stir-fry topped with almonds.

prep + cook time 15 minutes **serves** 4
nutritional count per serving 18.5g total fat (14g saturated fat); 267 cal; 17.6g carbohydrate; 4.6g protein; 6.5g fiber

tips Coconut oil is a solidified oil sold in jars and is available from major supermarkets and health food stores. Melt coconut oil as you would butter, either in a small saucepan over low heat or in the microwave. You will need about 1 bunch of water spinach for this recipe.

Fast-cooking clams are packed with a good dose of iron, B vitamins, and the mineral chronium, which the body needs to regulate blood glucose levels. They need to be soaked in salted water first to purge them of any sand.

spelt spaghetti with cherry tomato sauce and clams

You will need to soak the clams in salted water for 30 minutes before you start this recipe.

1 bunch fresh basil

2 pounds heirloom cherry tomatoes, halved

1 medium lemon, cut into 8 wedges

¼ cup olive oil

12 ounces spelt spaghetti

1 medium red onion, chopped finely

3 cloves garlic, sliced thinly

2 pounds clams

¾ cup dry white wine

1 Preheat oven to 400°F.

2 Pick leaves from bunch of basil; reserve 1 cup of the smallest leaves (keep remaining leaves for another use). Tie basil stalks together with kitchen string. Place tomatoes, lemon wedges, and basil stalks in a baking dish with 2 tablespoons of the oil; season, then toss to coat. Roast for 15 minutes or until tomatoes soften. Discard basil stalks. Squeeze juice from lemon wedges over tomatoes; discard wedges. Mash half the tomatoes with a fork.

3 Meanwhile, cook pasta in a large saucepan of boiling water or until almost tender.

4 Heat remaining oil in a large, deep frying pan over medium-high heat; cook onion and garlic, stirring, for 5 minutes or until softened. Add clams and wine; boil, stirring, for 1 minute. Cook, covered, for 5 minutes or until clams just open. Add tomato mixture, spaghetti, and three-quarters of the reserved basil leaves, then season; toss to combine.

5 Serve in bowls topped with remaining basil leaves.

prep + cook time 30 minutes **serves** 4
nutritional count per serving 15.4g total fat (2.3g saturated fat); 577 cal; 77.5g carbohydrate; 24g protein; 9g fiber

tips You can use whole-wheat spaghetti instead of the spelt spaghetti if you like. If you are a chile fan, simply add 1 fresh long finely chopped red chile with the onion in step 4.

Tomatoes contain the carotenoid lycopene, an antioxidant that gives them their red color, and may be useful in reducing the risk of some cancers and heart disease. While cooking does slightly reduce the vitamin C content in tomatoes, it actually increases the lycopene content.

roasted tomato and white bean soup

2 pounds ripe Roma tomatoes, quartered

1 medium red onion, cut into wedges

6 cloves garlic, unpeeled

1 tablespoon maple syrup

½ cup extra-virgin olive oil

⅓ cup loosely packed sage leaves

12½ ounces canned cannellini beans, drained, rinsed

2 cups water

1 Preheat oven to 400°F.

2 Place tomatoes, onion, and garlic in a roasting pan. Combine maple syrup and half the oil in a bowl, season to taste; pour over vegetables, then toss to coat. Roast for 45 minutes or until tomatoes are very soft and colored at the edges.

3 Meanwhile, heat remaining oil in a small frying pan over medium heat; fry sage leaves, stirring for 1½ minutes or until crisp. Remove with a slotted spoon; drain on paper towel. Reserve sage oil.

4 Peel roasted garlic. Blend garlic, onion, two-thirds of the tomatoes, and two-thirds of the beans until smooth. Pour mixture into a large saucepan with the water and remaining beans; cook over medium heat, stirring occasionally until warmed through. Season to taste.

5 Ladle soup into bowls. Top with remaining tomatoes and crisp sage leaves; drizzle with reserved sage oil.

prep + cook time 1 hour 10 minutes **serves** 4
nutritional count per serving 29g total fat (4.6g saturated fat); 381 cal; 18.9g carbohydrate; 7.6g protein; 8g fiber

A large number of quality scientific studies have provided strong evidence that consumption of brassica vegetables reduces the risk of cancer, particularly of the gastrointestinal tract and lungs.

THERE ARE BENEFITS TO CONSUMING BOTH RAW AND COOKED BRASSICAS. WHEN YOU COOK THEM YOU IMPROVE THE UPTAKE OF ANTIOXIDANTS INTO THE BLOODSTREAM FOR USE AROUND THE BODY. WHEN YOU CONSUME THE RAW VEG, MORE INTACT PLANT CELLS REACH THE COLON, WHERE THE RESIDENT BACTERIA BREAK THE CELLS DOWN, RELEASING THE ANTIOXIDANTS WHERE THEY CAN BENEFIT THE HEALTH OF COLONIC CELLS. RAW VEG MIGHT THEREFORE BE BETTER FOR REDUCING YOUR RISK OF BOWEL CANCER. WE THEREFORE RECOMMEND BOTH.

Eating

Eating brassicas regularly can help to protect you from other chronic diseases that affect us as we age, including Alzheimer's, cataracts, and age-related macular degeneration, and certain aspects of functional decline. Yes, eating more broccoli just might help keep you looking and feeling younger for longer.

Throw raw broccoli florets into your salad, or finely slice raw Brussels sprouts and cabbage to make a crunchy "slaw".

brassicas

Brassicas are a family of vegetables that include broccoli, broccolini, cauliflower, brussels sprouts, and cabbage (kale is also a brassica, but we've featured it on page 83). They deserve a superfood page all their own because they are especially protective against cancer and heart disease.

Lightly

Lightly steaming or stir-frying are the best ways to preserve the nutrients present in your veg. You can also throw them into dishes in the last few moments of cooking until just softened. Brassicas are best eaten in this way. If you cook them too long they won't taste very nice and they'll lose their bright green color.

How do

How do they do it? Brassicas are notably high in vitamins A, C, and E, folate, and potassium. All of these nutrients undoubtedly contribute toward the protective effect of these veggies. But it is the presence of particular phytochemicals that makes brassicas special. They contain a group of antioxidants called flavonoids, and a whole bunch of sulphur-containing compounds including glucosinolates, which act as anti-cancer agents and ramp up detoxifying enzyme systems.

Avocados are grown year round, with different varieties peaking at different times. One of the tastiest is hass, with creamy flesh, an oval shape and pebbly dark skin as it ripens. To check if avocados are ripe, squeeze the neck end gently.

chilled avocado soup with crab

3 fresh jalapeños or long green chiles

3 green onions (scallions), white and green parts

2 cloves garlic

¼ pound yellow grape tomatoes

2 tablespoons extra-virgin olive oil

¼ cup fresh cilantro, torn

¼ pound cooked fresh crab meat

⅓ cup lime juice

1 cup water

2 medium avocados, chopped

¾ cup Greek-style yogurt

1 Preheat oven to 400°F.

2 Cut two of the chiles in half lengthwise. Place in a roasting pan with the white part of onion, garlic, tomatoes, and half the oil, season with salt; toss to coat. Roast for 15 minutes or until chiles are soft. Cool.

3 Meanwhile, remove seeds from remaining chile; chop finely. Thinly slice the green part of the onion. Combine chopped chile, sliced green onion, cilantro, crab, and remaining oil in a medium bowl. Cover; refrigerate until ready to serve.

4 Blend roasted vegetables with juice, the water, avocado, and yogurt until smooth. Season to taste. Refrigerate until chilled.

5 Ladle chilled soup into bowls; top with crab mixture. Season with freshly ground black pepper.

prep + cook time 20 minutes (+ refrigeration)
serves 6 as a starter
nutritional count per serving 20.8g total fat (5g saturated fat); 245 cal; 6.3g carbohydrate; 6.4g protein; 2.8g fiber

tips If you want to reduce the intensity of the chiles, remove their seeds and membranes before roasting. You can use chopped prawns or diced scallops instead of the crab meat, if you like. You will need 3 limes for this recipe.

avocado pesto with prawns and pasta

¾ pound whole-wheat penne

¾ pound asparagus, trimmed, halved crosswise

2½ cups firmly packed fresh basil leaves, plus ⅓ cup lightly packed fresh small basil leaves

¼ cup pine nuts, toasted

1 clove garlic, crushed

2 tablespoons extra-virgin olive oil

¼ cup lemon juice

1 tablespoon water

1 medium avocado, chopped

¼ pound feta

2 pounds cooked tiger prawns (shrimp), shelled, deveined, with tails intact

1 Cook pasta in a large saucepan of boiling salted water for 8 minutes or until almost tender. Add asparagus; cook a further 1 minute until tender. Drain. Rinse under cold water; drain.
2 Meanwhile, process 2½ cups basil, pine nuts, garlic, oil, juice, and the water until finely chopped. Add avocado and half the feta; process until smooth. Season to taste.
3 Place pasta, asparagus, and pesto mixture in a large bowl with prawns; toss gently to combine.
4 Divide pasta among bowls; top with remaining feta and the small basil leaves.

prep + cook time 25 minutes **serves** 4
nutritional count per serving 37.2g total fat (10.2g saturated fat); 791 cal; 59.5g carbohydrate; 48g protein; 12.7g fiber

tip Asparagus spears vary in thickness; if the ends are really thick, peel them from the bottom up to within 2 inches of the tips.

sweet potato, eggplant, and coconut curry

1¼ pounds finger eggplants

olive oil spray

4 tablespoons olive oil

1 large onion, chopped finely

1½-inch piece fresh ginger, chopped finely

1 fresh small red chile, chopped finely

2 cloves garlic, crushed

4 cardamom pods, crushed lightly

1 teaspoon garam marsala

1 teaspoon ground cumin

1 teaspoon ground turmeric

1½ pounds orange sweet potatoes,
cut into 1¼-inch pieces

9 fluid ounces canned coconut milk

12½ ounces canned diced tomatoes

1 cup vegetable stock

1 tablespoon brown mustard seeds

24 fresh curry leaves

¾ pound lacinato kale, chopped coarsely

2 tablespoons water

1 Preheat oven to 350°F. Line two baking sheets with parchment paper.

2 Quarter eggplants lengthwise; place on baking sheets, spray with oil. Bake for 20 minutes or until golden and soft.

3 Heat 2 tablespoons olive oil in a large saucepan over medium-high heat; cook onion, ginger, chile, and garlic for 3 minutes. Reduce heat to low, add cardamom, garam marsala, cumin, and turmeric; cook for 2 minutes. Increase heat to medium, add sweet potato; stir to coat in spices.

4 Add coconut milk to pan with tomatoes and stock; bring to a boil. Reduce heat; simmer, covered, for 20 minutes or until sweet potato is tender. Stir in eggplant; return to a boil. Season to taste.

5 Meanwhile, heat remaining oil in a large frying pan over medium-high heat; cook mustard seeds, stirring, for 1 minute or until seeds pop. Add curry leaves; cook 1 minute. Stir in kale and the water; cook, covered, until just wilted. Season to taste.

6 Serve curry with cabbage mixture.

prep + cook time 1 hour **serves** 6
nutritional count per serving 23.6g total fat (10.2g saturated fat); 392 cal; 32.7g carbohydrate; 7.9g protein; 10g fiber

serving suggestion Serve with steamed basmati rice and yogurt.

Garlic stands out as having particularly potent anticancer effects. It has high levels of allicin and other sulphur compounds that are thought to be responsible. Garlic is also antibacterial; it can block the formation of carcinogenic substances, can enhance the repair of DNA in cells around the body, and can assist in killing off rogue cells that may progress to cancer. The World Health Organization recommends we eat a clove of garlic a day for general health.

Does cooking affect the benefits?

High heat, prolonged storage, and exposure to light are known to affect the levels and form of the potentially beneficial substances in garlic. But on the other hand, raw garlic disagrees with many people. You might find that raw garlic makes you burp, and garlic breath is not so desirable. Or you may find it causes heartburn or indigestion. Since there are many studies showing a benefit of cooked and raw garlic, as well as other cooked allium vegetables, there is clearly still a benefit from enjoying them in this way. What you might do is rather than frying your garlic at the start of the dish, try adding it a little later to the pan to reduce the heat exposure.

alliums

The alliums are the onion family of vegetables that includes onions, leeks, garlic, green onions (or scallions), spring onions, and shallots. These vegetables have been associated with a lower risk of several cancers, including cancer of the stomach, colon, esophagus, pancreas, breast, prostate, and brain.

You have no

doubt heard of probiotics—healthy bacteria that we need to colonize the gut—well, research suggests that prebiotics might be more important. These are compounds in food that act as specific fuel to these good bacteria. Having prebiotics in your diet therefore encourages the growth of healthy bacterial populations and pushes out the bad guys. Alliums provide a particular group of these prebiotics called fructooligosaccharides (FOS).

FRUCTOOLIGOSACCHARIDES (FOS) CAN CAUSE PROBLEMS FOR PEOPLE WITH IRRITABLE BOWEL DISEASE (IBS), BUT THAT MAY BE DUE TO HAVING AN IMBALANCE OF BACTERIAL GROUPS PRESENT, WITH MORE OF THE BAD GUYS. SEE A DIETITIAN OR OTHER HEALTH PROFESSIONAL FOR MORE ADVICE.

THE BOTTOM LINE is, however you enjoy alliums, get them into your daily menu. Use them in cooking, throw them raw into salads, or crush a clove of garlic into a salad dressing.

Numerous studies have shown that members of the brassica family, which includes cauliflower and lacinato kale, offer some protection against cancers, heart disease, and the functional declines associated with aging.

cauliflower and tomato gratin

¼ cup olive oil

2 pounds cauliflower, cut into small florets

2 medium onions, chopped finely

3 cloves garlic, crushed

½ teaspoon saffron threads

1½ pounds canned diced tomatoes

¼ cup currants

7 ounces lacinato kale, shredded

¼ cup coarsely chopped fresh flat-leaf parsley

topping

8 ounces spelt or whole-grain bread, torn coarsely

¼ cup pine nuts

¼ cup sunflower seeds

¼ cup pepitas (pumpkin seeds)

2 tablespoons sesame seeds

½ cup grated pecorino cheese

1 clove garlic, chopped

¼ cup olive oil

1 Heat 2 tablespoons of the oil in a large, deep frying pan over medium heat; cook cauliflower, covered, stirring occasionally, for 6 minutes or until starting to color. Remove from pan.
2 Heat remaining oil in same pan; cook onion and garlic, covered, for 3 minutes. Add saffron, tomatoes, and currants; bring to a simmer. Return cauliflower to pan with cabbage and parsley; cook, stirring, until cabbage just wilts. Season to taste.
3 Preheat oven to 350°F.
4 Make topping.
5 Spoon cauliflower mixture into a 3-quart ovenproof dish; cover evenly with topping mixture. Bake for 35 minutes or until topping is crisp and golden.
topping Combine ingredients in a medium bowl.

prep + cook time 1 hour **serves** 6
nutritional count per serving 35.7g total fat (5.8g saturated fat); 537 cal; 31.5g carbohydrate; 16.5g protein; 13.3g fiber

tip Pecorino is a hard Italian sheep's milk cheese similar to parmesan, which may be used instead, if you like.

spicy roast pumpkin with lamb

¾ cup cracked wheat

2 tablespoons coarsely chopped fresh flat-leaf parsley

2 tablespoons coarsely chopped fresh thyme,
plus 6 thyme sprigs, torn

2 tablespoons finely grated lemon zest

2 cloves garlic, crushed

2 tablespoons olive oil

2¾-pound small kabocha squash, unpeeled, cut into
small wedges

1 cup Greek-style yogurt

2 teaspoons sumac

lamb topping

1 tablespoon olive oil

1 medium onion, chopped finely

1 teaspoon ground cinnamon

½ teaspoon cayenne pepper

½ pound ground lamb

1 tablespoon pomegranate molasses

1 Cook cracked wheat in a medium saucepan of boiling water for 10 minutes (it will not be quite cooked). Drain; rinse. Place wheat in a medium bowl; cool for 15 minutes. Stir in chopped herbs, zest, garlic, and oil; season to taste.

2 Preheat oven to 350°F. Line a large baking sheet with parchment paper.

3 Place squash wedges, skin-side down, on baking sheet; spoon wheat mixture into the hollow of each wedge. Bake, uncovered, for 30 minutes; cover with foil, bake a further 30 minutes or until squash is tender.

4 Meanwhile, make lamb topping.

5 Spoon lamb topping over squash wedges; serve topped with yogurt, sumac, and thyme sprigs.

lamb topping Heat oil in a frying pan over medium heat; cook onion, cinnamon, and cayenne, stirring for 3 minutes. Increase heat to high, add lamb; cook, stirring occasionally, for 5 minutes or until browned and cooked through. Stir in molasses; season to taste.

prep + cook time 1 hour 30 minutes **serves** 6
nutritional count per serving 19.8g total fat (6g saturated fat);
442 cal; 42g carbohydrate; 18.9g protein; 10.3g fiber

seeded carrot and cabbage filo pie

½ cup olive oil

1 small leek, white part only, sliced thinly

2 cloves garlic, crushed

2 teaspoons caraway seeds

2 medium carrots, grated coarsely

½ pound savoy cabbage, shredded

¼ cup currants

2 tablespoons finely chopped fresh mint

14 sheets filo pastry

topping

¼ cup pepitas (pumpkin seeds)

¼ cup slivered almonds

¼ cup coarsely chopped walnuts

1 tablespoon poppyseeds

1 tablespoon sesame seeds

herb salad

2 small Persian cucumbers

1 cup fresh flat-leaf parsley leaves

1 cup fresh curly parsley leaves

½ cup fresh mint leaves

½ cup fresh dill sprigs

2 green onions (scallions), sliced thinly

1 tablespoon red wine vinegar

2 tablespoons olive oil

2½ ounces soft goat cheese, crumbled

1 Heat ¼ cup oil in a large frying pan over medium heat; cook leek, garlic, and seeds for 5 minutes. Add carrot; cook for 3 minutes. Add cabbage; cook a further 5 minutes or until vegetables are soft. Stir in currants and mint. Cool.
2 Make topping.
3 Preheat oven to 350°F.
4 Divide filling into seven portions. Brush one sheet of pastry with a little of the remaining oil; top with a second sheet. Keep remaining sheets covered with a clean, damp tea towel. Place one portion of filling lengthwise, in a thin line, along pastry edge; roll pastry over filling. Starting at the center of a 9½-inch springform pan, carefully form the pastry roll, seam-side down, into a coil. Repeat with remaining pastry, oil, and filling, joining each roll to the end of the last one and coiling it around until the base of the pan is covered. Brush top with oil.
5 Bake filo pie for 18 minutes. Evenly cover with topping; bake a further 8 minutes or until golden.
6 Meanwhile, make herb salad.
7 Serve filo pie with herb salad.
topping Combine ingredients in a small bowl.
herb salad Using a vegetable peeler, peel cucumbers into ribbons. Place cucumber in a medium bowl with herbs, onion, vinegar, and oil; toss gently to combine. Top with cheese.

prep + cook time 1 hour **serves** 6
nutritional count per serving 30.9g total fat (5.5g saturated fat); 485 cal; 33.8g carbohydrate; 13.5g protein; 10.4g fiber

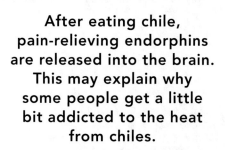

After eating chile, pain-relieving endorphins are released into the brain. This may explain why some people get a little bit addicted to the heat from chiles.

HALF A BELL PEPPER PROVIDES A GOOD DOSE OF FOLATE, ABOUT 7% OF YOUR DAILY NEED, AND ROUGHLY 8% OF YOUR VITAMIN B6. BOTH OF THESE VITAMINS ARE INVOLVED IN REDUCING BLOOD LEVELS OF THE AMINO ACID HOMOCYSTEINE. RAISED HOMOCYSTEINE HAS BEEN ASSOCIATED WITH AN INCREASED RISK OF CARDIOVASCULAR DISEASE. VITAMIN B6 IS ALSO NECESSARY FOR PROTEIN METABOLISM, HEALTHY RADIANT SKIN, AND GOOD IMMUNE FUNCTION.

bell pepper & chile

The chemical responsible for heat of a spicy chile is capsaicin. This fiery little compound has many potential benefits in the body. It increases the body's production of heat and can help to clear nasal congestion, making it a great winter food. Capsaicin may also be able to kill off rogue cancer cells and help to detoxify cancer-causing agents.

It's not only oranges that are fabulous for vitamin C, half a red bell pepper gives you well over your entire daily requirement. Vitamin C is one of the major antioxidants and an essential player in supporting optimal immune function.

Peppers also provide an array of carotenoids, including beta-carotene, with antioxidant functions. Some can also be converted to vitamin A in the body, a nutrient that is critical for good vision and healthy eyes. Since it is also necessary for new cell formation, vitamin A is essential for healthy skin and many organs including the heart, lungs, liver, and kidneys.

Toasting nuts and seeds amplifies their flavor and will freshen them up if they're a little on the stale side. Toast the sesame seeds in a heavy-bottomed frying pan without any oil over medium heat, stirring continuously, for 3 minutes or until they're evenly golden.

broccoli and ocean trout salad

1¼ pounds broccoli florets

2 tablespoons olive oil

¾ brussels sprouts, halved

3 green onions (scallions), sliced thinly

½ cup dry-roasted cashews, chopped coarsely

1 tablespoon sesame seeds, toasted

1 medium Asian pear, cored, sliced thinly

7-ounce skinless, boneless ocean trout fillet

2 tablespoons rice flour or cornstarch

2 tablespoons peanut oil

dressing

1 tablespoon sesame oil

1 tablespoon olive oil

¼ cup rice wine vinegar

1 clove garlic, crushed

¼ teaspoon cayenne pepper

1 tablespoon soy sauce

1 Make dressing.

2 Cook broccoli in a large saucepan of boiling water 1 minute; drain. Refresh under cold water; drain. Pat broccoli dry with paper towels.

3 Heat half the olive oil in a large frying pan over medium-high heat; cook sprouts, cut-side down, for 2 minutes or until golden. Turn over; cook a further minute or until almost tender. Remove from pan.

4 Heat remaining oil in same frying pan; cook broccoli for 3 minutes or until browned lightly and warmed.

5 Place sprouts and broccoli in a large bowl with onion, nuts, sesame seeds, pear, and dressing; toss gently to combine.

6 Cut trout into ½-inch slices. Dust slices in rice flour; shake off excess. Heat peanut oil in same frying pan over high heat; cook trout for 1 minute each side or until golden and cooked through. Drain on paper towels.

7 Serve salad topped with flaked pieces of trout.

dressing Place ingredients in a screw-top jar; shake well.

prep + cook time 35 minutes serves 6
nutritional count per serving 30.1g total fat (5g saturated fat); 382 cal; 9.9g carbohydrate; 14.1g protein; 6.6g fiber

Beet stems are tender and sweet like chard, and the slightly sour leaves are also edible. Little is wasted in this clever tart that utilizes all parts of the beet.

roasted beet, garlic, and chia seed tart

1 pound baby beet, stems and leaves attached

8 cloves garlic, unpeeled, plus 1 clove garlic, crushed

6 sprigs fresh thyme

2½ tablespoons olive oil

3 medium red onions, sliced thinly

2 ounces soft goat cheese, crumbled

2 tablespoons extra-virgin olive oil

2 tablespoons orange juice

1 teaspoon white chia seeds

pastry

2 tablespoons white chia seeds

2 tablespoons warm water

1½ cups whole-wheat flour

1 teaspoon sea salt flakes

1½ ounces cold unsalted butter, chopped

1 egg

¼ cup olive oil

1 Trim beets, leaving a little of the stems attached. Finely chop enough of the stems to make up 2 tablespoons; reserve for the pastry. Pick ¾ ounce small beet leaves, cover with damp paper towel; refrigerate until ready to use. Pick a further 3 ounces of beet leaves, shred finely; refrigerate. Discard remaining leaves and stems.

2 Make pastry.

3 Preheat oven to 400°F. Line a baking sheet with foil.

4 Place beets, unpeeled garlic, and thyme in the center of the baking sheet; drizzle with 2 teaspoons of the oil. Wrap foil around beets. Roast 20 minutes; check garlic, remove if tender when lightly squeezed. Roast beets a further 10 minutes or until tender; discard thyme. Peel beets; cut into quarters.

5 Meanwhile, heat remaining oil in a large frying pan over low heat; cook onions, stirring occasionally, for 20 minutes or until very soft. Add shredded leaves; stir for 3 minutes or until wilted. Season to taste. Cool.

6 Roll pastry between sheets of parchment paper into a 12-inch round. Using a bowl as a guide, trim pastry into a 11¾-inch round. Fold in the edge to create a ½-inch border.

7 Slide pastry with the paper onto a large baking sheet; bake for 12 minutes or until golden. Spread onion mixture on tart base; top with roasted beets and garlic and cheese. Bake a further 10 minutes or until cheese is golden.

8 Whisk crushed garlic, extra-virgin olive oil, and juice in a small bowl; season to taste. Add reserved small beet leaves; toss to coat. Top tart with beet leaves; sprinkle with chia seeds.

pastry Combine chia seeds and the water in a medium bowl; let stand for 20 minutes. Add flour, salt, and butter; rub together until mixture resembles coarse crumbs. Stir in reserved beet stems (from step 1). Whisk egg and oil in a small bowl, add to flour mixture; mix with your hands until just combined. Shape pastry into a disc. Cover; refrigerate 30 minutes.

prep + cook time 1 hour 15 minutes (+ standing & refrigeration)
serves 4
nutritional count per serving 54g total fat (15.2g saturated fat); 802 cal; 54.1g carbohydrate; 17.8g protein; 17.4g fiber

tip You could also use 2 bunches of small beets. You will need to roast them for 1¼ hours and cut them into wedges.

super seafood

An abundance of scientific research shows the benefits of eating more fish and seafood in our diet.

You can use four 8-ounce pieces of salmon fillet instead of the barramundi, if you like. You will need to reduce the cooking time slightly.

baked baby barramundi with pumpkin seed pesto

1 pound asparagus

½ pound green beans

4 x 11-ounce plate-size barramundi

2 medium lemons, sliced thinly

¼ cup olive oil

pumpkin seed pesto

1 cup pepitas (pumpkin seeds)

2 cups firmly packed fresh basil leaves

1 clove garlic, crushed

1 tablespoon finely grated lemon zest

¼ cup lemon juice

⅓ cup olive oil

¼ cup water

1 Preheat oven to 425°F. Line two large baking sheets with parchment paper.

2 Divide asparagus and beans between baking sheets. Cut three slashes crosswise into the thickest part of each fish on both sides; place on vegetables. Top fish with lemon slices, drizzle with olive oil; season.

3 Bake fish and vegetables for 25 minutes or until fish is cooked through (the flesh in the slits will appear opaque).

4 Meanwhile, make Pumpkin Seed Pesto.

5 Divide fish and vegetables among plates; serve with pesto.

pumpkin seed pesto Process pepitas, basil, garlic, zest, and juice until well combined. With the motor operating, gradually add combined oil and the water; process until smooth.

prep + cook time 40 minutes **serves** 4

nutritional count per serving 57.1g total fat (9.3g saturated fat); 788 cal; 11g carbohydrate; 54.2g protein; 9.5g fiber

tip If you have both pans in the oven at the same time, to ensure even cooking, either swap the pans halfway through cooking time or use the oven's convection function (you will need to reduce the temperature to 400°F).

Sashimi-grade fish must be impeccably fresh and prepared using extremely strict standards of hygiene as the fish is to be eaten raw. If you are unable to obtain it, or prefer your fish cooked, simply cook the fish for a further 1½ minutes on each side or until cooked through.

seared wasabi salmon and brown rice salad

1 pound packaged pre-cooked brown basmati rice

¾ pound sashimi-grade salmon

2 tablespoons sesame seeds

1 tablespoon wasabi powder

3 tablespoons olive oil

3 ounces baby Asian salad leaves

¼ cup pickled ginger

2 green onions (scallions), sliced thinly

1 fresh long red chile, sliced thinly

1 large avocado, chopped

2 tablespoons light soy sauce

2 tablespoons lime juice

1 lime, cut into wedges

1 Reheat rice following packet instructions; cool slightly.
2 Meanwhile, roll salmon in combined sesame seeds and wasabi powder until coated.
3 Heat 2 tablespoons oil in a large frying pan over high heat; cook salmon for 1 minute each side or until browned but still raw in the center. Cool for 5 minutes. Cut into thin slices.
4 Place brown rice in a large bowl with salad leaves, ginger, onion, chile, and avocado; toss gently to combine.
5 Place sauce, juice, and remaining 1 tablespoon oil in a screw-top jar; shake well.
6 Arrange rice salad and salmon on a platter; drizzle with dressing. Serve with lime wedges.

prep + cook time 20 minutes **serves** 4
nutritional count per serving 41.6g total fat (8.4g saturated fat); 691 cal; 44.3g carbohydrate; 32g protein; 5.4g fiber

tips If you can't find wasabi powder, use the equivalent amount of wasabi paste and spread it over the salmon before rolling it in sesame seeds.

SALMON IS ALSO RICH IN PROTEIN AND A NEW AREA OF RESEARCH IS LOOKING AT THE POTENTIAL BENEFITS OF SOME OF THE PEPTIDES (SMALL PROTEINS) PRESENT. ONE IN PARTICULAR CALLED CALCITONIN IS GARNERING A LOT OF ATTENTION. WE MAKE OUR OWN FORM OF CALCITONIN IN THE THYROID GLAND, AND WE KNOW IT'S INVOLVED IN COLLAGEN FORMATION AND BONE METABOLISM. THIS NEW RESEARCH IS INVESTIGATING WHETHER THE CALCITONIN AND OTHER BIOACTIVE PEPTIDES IN SALMON MAY HAVE BENEFITS IN MAINTAINING HEALTHY JOINTS AND BONES AND SLOWING THE AGING OF THE SKIN. SALMON JUST MIGHT HELP TO KEEP US LOOKING YOUNGER.

The long-chain omega-3 fats are anti-inflammatory and so can be useful in treating arthritis, and may help to control asthma by lowering inflammation in the lungs. Salmon may have additional anti-inflammatory factors that make it a particularly "super" food. It is one of the best sources of selenium, and high intakes of this mineral have been associated with decreased risk of joint inflammation, as well as a lower risk of several types of cancer.

Omega-3s are good for your heart. They lower blood triglyceride levels and blood pressure.

atlantic salmon

Atlantic salmon ranks amongt the richest food sources of the long-chain omega-3 fats EPA and DHA. Salmon is especially rich in DHA, the most abundant omega-3 fat in the brain and in the retina of the eye. DHA is therefore considered to be particularly important for brain function and general brain health.

Cultures that eat a lot of fish and seafood have lower levels of depression. There is ongoing research into this area, but there is certainly some evidence to suggest that upping the intake of omega-3s can help reduce depressive symptoms in some people.

Although we can make EPA and DHA from shorter chain omega-3 fats found in some plants, our capacity to do this is limited. To ensure we get optimal amounts, we really need to consume sufficient amounts in our diet. To meet requirements, our health recommendations are to consume oily fish such as salmon at least a couple of times a week.

Harissa is a spicy North African condiment of chile and spices. Recent research has shown countries with a high chile consumption, such as Mexico and India, tend to have decreased rates of cancer. Chiles also boost our metabolism, helping to burn fat and increase satiety.

harissa and tomato shrimp with feta

1 tablespoon plus 2 teaspoons olive oil

1 medium onion, sliced thinly

2 cloves garlic, sliced thinly

¼ cup dry white wine

20 uncooked shrimp, shelled, deveined, with tails intact

2 teaspoons harissa

12½ ounces canned diced tomatoes

2 tablespoons currants

1 teaspoon caster (superfine) sugar

2 cups whole-wheat couscous

2 cups boiling water

3 ounces Greek feta, crumbled

2 tablespoons fresh flat-leaf parsley leaves

1 Preheat broiler to high.

2 Heat 1 tablespoon oil in a large, deep, ovenproof frying pan over medium heat; cook onion and garlic for 5 minutes or until tender. Add wine; cook over high heat for 30 seconds. Add shrimp and harissa; cook, stirring occasionally, for 2 minutes. Add tomatoes, currants, and sugar. Reduce heat to low; cook for 3 minutes or until shrimp are just cooked. Season.

3 Meanwhile, place couscous and the boiling water in a large bowl. Cover with plastic wrap; stand for 5 minutes or until water is absorbed. Fluff couscous with a fork.

4 Scatter feta on shrimp; drizzle with 2 teaspoons oil. Place pan under broiler for 2 minutes or until feta is golden. Sprinkle with parsley. Serve shrimp with couscous.

prep + cook time 25 minutes **serves** 4
nutritional count per serving 14.5g total fat (5g saturated fat); 637 cal; 89g carbohydrate; 34.8g protein; 2.8g fiber

tips If you don't like things too spicy, replace 1 teaspoon of harissa with 1 teaspoon cumin seeds. If you don't have an ovenproof frying pan, wrap the handle of your pan in several layers of foil.

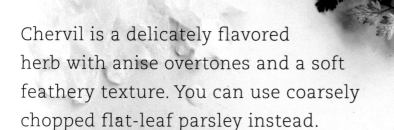

Chervil is a delicately flavored herb with anise overtones and a soft feathery texture. You can use coarsely chopped flat-leaf parsley instead.

oysters with cucumber and shallot salad

1 Persian cucumber, halved lengthwise

1 shallot, chopped finely

2 tablespoons champagne vinegar

1 teaspoon caster (superfine) sugar

2 tablespoons fresh chervil leaves

24 oysters on the half shell

1 Scrape out the seeds from the cucumber using a teaspoon; finely chop the cucumber.

2 Combine cucumber, shallot, vinegar, sugar, and half the chervil in a small bowl.

3 Spoon salad onto oysters; top with remaining chervil.

prep time 10 minutes **serves** 4 as a starter

nutritional count per serving 1.4g total fat (0.4g saturated fat); 56 cal; 2.2g carbohydrate; 7.5g protein; 0.7g fiber

tip You can use white balsamic vinegar instead of the champagne vinegar.

You can take a recipe shortcut by chopping the mint and parsley in the food processor; just make sure you use the pulse button. For those with a gluten intolerance, replace the wheat with 1 cup cooked quinoa, brown rice, or millet.

baked salmon fillets
with tahini sauce and tabbouleh

4 x 4½-ounce salmon fillets, skinned

1½ teaspoons sumac

2 tablespoons extra-virgin olive oil

tabbouleh

½ cup coarse cracked wheat

1½ cups water

2 green onions (scallions), sliced thinly

1 medium tomato, chopped coarsely

1 cup firmly packed fresh flat-leaf parsley leaves, chopped coarsely

¼ cup firmly packed fresh mint leaves, chopped coarsely

1 tablespoon lemon juice

tahini sauce

½ cup Greek-style yogurt

1½ tablespoons tahini

1 clove garlic, crushed

2 teaspoons lemon juice

1 Make Tabbouleh, then Tahini Sauce.

2 Preheat oven to 400°F.

3 Line a baking sheet with parchment paper. Place salmon on baking sheet, sprinkle with 1 teaspoon of the sumac; drizzle with oil. Season. Bake for 12 minutes or until almost cooked through.

4 Serve salmon with tahini sauce and tabbouleh. Sprinkle with remaining sumac.

tabbouleh Bring cracked wheat and the water to a boil in a small saucepan. Reduce heat to low; cook for 20 minutes or until tender. Drain. Place cracked wheat in a large bowl with onion, tomato, herbs, and juice; toss to combine. Season.

tahini sauce Whisk ingredients in a small bowl until combined; season to taste.

prep + cook time 40 minutes **serves** 4
nutritional count per serving 35.3g total fat (8.4g saturated fat); 602 cal; 18.9g carbohydrate; 49.3g protein; 6g fiber

tip You can make the tabbouleh and tahini sauce several hours ahead; store in the refrigerator until ready to use.

Shellfish are rich in selenium—a mineral we need only tiny amounts of, but is often lacking in our diets due to low selenium levels in the soil. Selenium is necessary for thyroid hormone metabolism, to make DNA, and to protect cells around the body from oxidative damage and infection.

If you don't like oysters, mussels and clams are not too far behind on the zinc front and are also iron rich—clams in particular are fantastic for iron. For those who choose not to eat red meat, tuck into shellfish on a regular basis to ensure you meet your body's requirement for both zinc and iron.

mussels, oysters & clams

The richest food source of zinc is oysters. Just one oyster provides approximately 10mg. The recommended intake for women is 8mg and men 14mg. It's not often our requirement for a mineral can be so easily met with a mouthful or two of one food.

A DOZEN MUSSELS PROVIDE ALL THE IRON AND VITAMIN B12 YOU NEED FOR THE DAY, A THIRD OF YOUR ZINC, MORE THAN A THIRD OF YOUR MAGNESIUM, AND A TENTH OF YOUR VITAMIN A. AND ALL FOR ONLY 129 CALORIES AND PRETTY MUCH NO SATURATED FAT. MOST OF THOSE CALORIES COME FROM PROTEIN, SO OPTING FOR MUSSELS ON THE MENU CAN HELP WITH CURBING YOUR APPETITE AND CONTROLLING YOUR WEIGHT.

Sustainable choices

From a seafood sustainability point of view, mussels, oysters, and other shellfish are considered some of the best choices.

Only "true" tarragon, the French variety, has a lovely anise-like flavor that pairs well with seafood. Although rarely labeled, French tarragon has distinguishing narrow leaves, while Russian tarragon has serrated leaves and yellow flowers. If unavailable, increase the dill to ½ cup.

shrimp, pea, and fava bean frittata with lemon herb salad

½ cup fresh flat-leaf parsley leaves

⅓ cup fresh dill sprigs

¼ cup fresh tarragon leaves

6 eggs

½ cup buttermilk

2 tablespoons dried breadcrumbs

1 pound cooked medium shrimp

2 tablespoons olive oil

2 medium zucchini, halved lengthwise, sliced thinly

3 green onions (scallions), sliced thinly

2 cloves garlic, crushed

2 cups frozen peas, thawed

2¼ cups frozen fava beans, peeled, thawed

⅓ cup ricotta

1 medium lemon, segmented (see tip)

1 tablespoon baby salted capers, rinsed

1 Coarsely chop half the herbs. Reserve remaining herbs. Whisk chopped herbs, eggs, buttermilk, and breadcrumbs in a large bowl; season.

2 Shell and devein shrimp, leaving 6 shrimp with tails intact.

3 Preheat oven to 350°F.

4 Heat oil in an 8½-inch ovenproof frying pan over medium heat; cook zucchini and onion, stirring, for 5 minutes or until soft. Add garlic, peas, and beans; cook, stirring, for 1 minute or until fragrant. Add egg mixture; gently shake pan to distribute mixture. Cook over medium-low heat, without stirring, for 5 minutes or until the edge is set. Add shrimp, placing shrimp with tails upright in pan. Top with ricotta. Bake frittata for 20 minutes or until the center is just firm.

5 Meanwhile, combine reserved herbs, lemon segments, and capers in a small bowl.

6 Serve frittata topped with lemon herb salad.

prep + cook time 1 hour **serves** 4
nutritional count per serving 20.6g total fat (5.6g saturated fat); 414 cal; 15.8g carbohydrate; 35.8g protein; 10.4g fiber

tips If you don't have an ovenproof frying pan, wrap the handle of your pan in several layers of foil. To segment a lemon, use a small sharp knife to cut the top and bottom from lemon. Cut off the zest with the white pith, following the curve of the fruit. Holding the lemon over a bowl, cut down both sides of the white membrane to release each segment.

A fish burger makes a delicious alternative to a beef burger and is a particularly good way to disguise fish for finicky eaters. You can use white-fleshed fish, or even shrimp, instead of the salmon for something different.

salmon and zucchini burgers with green hummus

1 medium zucchini, grated coarsely

¼ teaspoon salt

1-pound skinless, boneless salmon fillet, chopped coarsely

6 green onions (scallions), chopped finely

2 cloves garlic, crushed

1 egg

1 teaspoon ground cumin

⅓ cup coarsely chopped fresh mint

⅓ cup coarsely chopped fresh flat-leaf parsley

⅓ cup coarsely chopped fresh dill

⅔ cup coarse fresh whole-wheat breadcrumbs

½ cup hummus

2 tablespoon Greek-style yogurt

2 tablespoons olive oil

½ baby romaine lettuce

2 medium tomatoes, sliced thinly

4 whole-grain bread rolls, split, toasted

1 Combine zucchini and salt in a small bowl; stand 5 minutes. Squeeze excess liquid from zucchini.

2 Pulse salmon in a food processor into ½-inch pieces. Add zucchini, onion, garlic, egg, cumin, and half the herbs; pulse until well combined (pulse in short quick bursts to ensure you don't overmix and make the mixture tough). Add breadcrumbs, pulse until combined; season. (The mixture will be quite wet but will firm on chileng.) Using damp hands, shape mixture into four 4-inch patties. Place on a baking sheet lined with parchment paper. Cover; refrigerate 30 minutes.

3 Meanwhile, to make green hummus, process hummus and remaining herbs in processor until smooth. Add yogurt; pulse until combined.

4 Heat oil in a large frying pan over medium heat; cook patties for 3 minutes each side or until just cooked through.

5 Place lettuce, patties, green hummus, and tomato between toasted rolls.

prep + cook time 40 minutes (+ refrigeration) **serves** 4
nutritional count per serving 33.8g total fat (7.4g saturated fat); 593 cal; 22.4g carbohydrate; 46g protein; 7.6g fiber

tip To make ⅔ cup fresh breadcrumbs, remove the crust from three ¾-inch thick slices of whole-wheat bread; process slices until they become coarse crumbs.

Cooking the fish next to the bay leaves will infuse it with a camphor-like flavor. You could also use citrus-scented kaffir lime leaves for an Asian flavor and continue the theme to the coleslaw by swapping pecans with peanuts, lemon juice with lime juice, and parsley with cilantro.

snapper and bay leaf skewers with root vegetable slaw

You will need to soak 8 bamboo skewers in water for about an hour before you start this recipe.

½ medium celeriac (celery root), peeled

1 medium red apple, unpeeled

1 medium carrot, unpeeled

8 ounces savoy cabbage, shredded finely

⅔ cup finely chopped fresh chives

¼ cup chopped fresh flat-leaf parsley

⅓ cup pecans, roasted, chopped coarsely

⅓ cup buttermilk

⅓ cup extra-virgin olive oil

2 teaspoons lemon juice

2 pounds thick snapper fillets, skinned, trimmed

24 large fresh bay leaves

1 tablespoon olive oil

1 medium lemon, cut into wedges

1 To make slaw, using a mandoline or V-slicer, slice celeriac, apple, and carrot into matchsticks. Place sliced vegetables in a large bowl with cabbage, herbs, and nuts. Add combined buttermilk, extra-virgin olive oil and juice, then season; toss gently to combine.

2 Cut snapper into 16 even pieces (about 2 inches each) avoiding any bones. Thread 3 bay leaves and 2 pieces of snapper alternately onto each skewer. Brush snapper with olive oil; season.

3 Cook skewers on a heated grill pan (or under a broiler or on a grill) over medium heat for 2 minutes each side or until just cooked through.

4 Serve skewers with slaw and lemon wedges.

prep + cook time 45 minutes **serves** 4
nutritional count per serving 34.6g total fat (6g saturated fat); 600 cal; 13g carbohydrate; 55g protein; 8g fiber

tip Leftover slaw will keep well for up to 2 days in the fridge.

Both shrimp

and octopus provide good levels of the long-chain omega-3 fats you might be taking as a fish oil supplement. These fats are crucially important in the brain and seem to play a role in cognitive function and brain health as we age. In children, these fats are essential for optimal brain development.

OMEGA-3

FATS ARE ANTI-INFLAMMATORY AND THEREFORE CAN BE HELPFUL IN RELIEVING ALL SORTS OF INFLAMMATORY CONDITIONS, INCLUDING ARTHRITIS, BUT MAY ALSO HELP TO REDUCE THE LOW-GRADE INFLAMMATION THAT OCCURS ALONGSIDE MANY CHRONIC DISEASES AND OBESITY.

shrimp & octopus

Try throwing some octopus on your grill for a change. 3 ounces of cooked octopus has more than double the iron content of a similar amount of steak, but has 30% fewer calories, hardly any fat, and delivers a similar amount of protein. Octopus is also fabulously rich in vitamin B6, vitamin B12, phosphorus, copper, and selenium.

For years people worried about the cholesterol found in shrimp. However, today we understand much more about what dietary factors affect our blood cholesterol profile. Dietary cholesterol is a minor factor. In fact, in most of us the more cholesterol we eat the less our liver makes, and vice versa. If you have a poor cholesterol profile, concentrate on changing the types of fats in your diet rather than worrying about cholesterol in foods.

Octopus

that comes from Alaska is the recommended sustainable choice, with British Columbia and Hawaii good alternatives. Avoid octopus from Indonesia, the Philippines, and the Gulf of Mexico, as well as any caught by bottom trawls in Spain, Morocco, and Portugal.

Italian vincotto, literally meaning "cooked wine", is a condiment made from boiling down grape must (skins, seeds, and stems of grapes) until thick and syrupy. It is available from selected supermarkets and delis. You can use balsamic glaze instead.

baked sardines with fig and pine nut stuffing

⅔ cup chopped dried figs

⅓ cup red wine vinegar

⅓ cup olive oil

1 cup coarsely torn whole-wheat sourdough breadcrumbs

1 medium red onion, chopped finely

2 cloves garlic, crushed

2 teaspoons finely grated lemon zest

2 tablespoons chopped fresh rosemary, plus 2 tablespoons intact fresh rosemary leaves

2 tablespoons chopped fresh flat-leaf parsley

2 tablespoons pine nuts, toasted

1 tablespoon lemon juice

12 sardines, butterflied, with tails intact

1 medium fennel bulb, trimmed, sliced

1 medium radicchio, cut into 12 wedges

2 tablespoons vincotto

1 Preheat oven to 400°F.

2 Combine figs and vinegar in a small saucepan over medium heat; simmer for 1 minute. Remove from heat; stand 10 minutes or until liquid is absorbed.

3 Meanwhile, heat 1 tablespoon of the oil in a large frying pan over medium heat; cook breadcrumbs, stirring, for 5 minutes or until golden. Remove from pan.

4 Heat another 1 tablespoon of the oil in same cleaned pan; cook onion, stirring, for 5 minutes or until soft. Add garlic, zest, and chopped rosemary; cook, stirring, for 1 minute or until fragrant. Remove pan from heat; stir in parsley, breadcrumbs, pine nuts, soaked figs, and juice. Season to taste.

5 Place sardines, in a single layer, in a large oiled ovenproof dish. Place a heaping tablespoon of stuffing mixture inside each sardine cavity, fold sardines over slightly to enclose filling. Top with any remaining stuffing mixture and whole rosemary leaves; drizzle with another 1 tablespoon of oil. Season. Bake for 15 minutes or until sardines are just cooked.

6 Meanwhile, brush fennel and radicchio with remaining oil; season. Cook fennel slices on a grill pan over medium heat for 2 minutes each side or until charred lightly; transfer to a platter. Cook radicchio wedges on grill plate for 1 minute each side or until charred lightly and tender. Add radicchio to fennel; drizzle with half the vincotto.

7 Drizzle sardines with remaining vincotto. Serve with fennel and radicchio.

prep + cook time 1 hour **serves** 6
nutritional count per serving 24.2g total fat (4.3g saturated fat); 411 cal; 23.3g carbohydrate; 22.3g protein; 5.9g fiber

tip For the breadcrumbs, it's best to use day-old or stale bread.

mussels, sweet potato, chickpeas, and greens in korma sauce

2 tablespoons olive oil

1 medium leek, white part only, sliced

2 cloves garlic, crushed

⅓ cup korma paste

9½ ounces orange sweet potato, diced

9 fluid ounces coconut milk

1 cup fish stock

12½ ounces canned diced tomatoes

1½ pounds canned chickpeas, drained, rinsed

2 pounds black mussels, scrubbed, bearded

½ pound baby spinach

½ cup fresh cilantro leaves

1 Heat oil in a large saucepan over medium-high heat; cook leek and garlic, stirring for 2 minutes or until softened.
2 Add korma paste to pan; cook, stirring, for 2 minutes. Add sweet potato, coconut milk, stock, tomatoes, and chickpeas; bring to a boil. Reduce heat; simmer for 6 minutes or until sweet potato is tender. Stir in mussels; cook, covered, for 4 minutes or until mussels open. Stir in spinach until wilted.
3 Serve mussels scattered with cilantro.

prep + cook time 35 minutes **serves** 4
nutritional count per serving 36.6g total fat (15.4g saturated fat); 623 cal; 41.9g carbohydrate; 25.5g protein; 12.8g fiber

serving suggestion Serve with steamed basmati rice.

This agrodolce (sweet and sour) Italian recipe uses currants and grapes for sweetness and vinegar for sourness. This traditional pairing of sour and sweet as a sauce or flavoring is thought to have been brought to Sicily by the Arabs.

whiting with pine nuts, currants, and lacinato kale

¼ cup plus 1½ tablespoons olive oil

1 medium red onion, halved, sliced thinly

1 cup small red grapes, halved

2 tablespoons currants

½ pound lacinato kale, trimmed, chopped coarsely

¼ cup red wine vinegar

⅓ cup pine nuts, toasted

8 sand whiting fillets (2 pounds) (see tip)

1 Heat ¼ cup olive oil in a large deep frying pan over medium-high heat; cook onion for 4 minutes or until softened. Add grapes and currants; cook, for 1 minute. Add kale and vinegar; cook, tossing, for 1 minute or until cabbage is just wilted. Add pine nuts.

2 Heat remaining oil in a large, frying pan over medium-high heat; cook fish, in two batches, for 1½ minutes each side or until just cooked through.

3 Serve fish on kale mixture.

prep + cook time 25 minutes **serves** 4
nutritional count per serving 30.5g total fat (4.1g saturated fat); 484 cal; 14.4g carbohydrate; 36.2g protein; 4.5g fiber

tip King George whiting is a delicately textured fish with a fine flake and, as is generally the case with small fish, it is a sustainable choice. You can use any other small white-fleshed fish such as snapper, bream, john dory, or mirror dory.

ONE OF OUR

CURRENT KEY ENVIRONMENTAL CONCERNS IS THE OVERFISHING OF OUR WATERS. FOR A NUTRITIONIST, IT IS SOMETHING OF A DILEMMA. FROM A NUTRITIONAL PERSPECTIVE, THERE IS NO DOUBT OF THE ENORMOUS BENEFITS OF EATING MORE FISH, BUT FROM AN ENVIRONMENTAL PERSPECTIVE WE CANNOT CONTINUE TO TAKE MORE FISH THAN CAN REPOPULATE.

Fish are a valuable source of vitamin B12, as well as small but useful amounts of iron and zinc.

White fish is an

excellent source of iodine. A 3-ounce snapper fillet, for example, provides you with more than a quarter of your daily requirement. Iodine is essential for the production of thyroid hormones that control metabolism. White fish also provide two minerals involved in many biological processed in the body including bone health— manganese and phosphorus. A serving of white fish can provide about a third of your daily manganese requirement and over three-quarters the daily requirement of phosphorus.

small fish

While large, oily fish often get all the nutritional kudos, small white fish are equally worthy of superfood status. Although they don't contain the same high levels of omega-3 fats (with the exception of sardines), they do provide a wealth of other nutrients. They are protein rich, with a 3-ounce fillet providing you with about 20g of high quality protein (i.e. it contains all the essential amino acids we need), and with very little fat the calorie count is far lower.

One of the solutions to concerns of overfishing is to take greater care regarding which fish we buy. We can learn which fish are at risk from overfishing and ensure we buy from fisheries with sound sustainability practices in place. Of course, your local fishmonger is likely to always have that information. One factor to consider is the size of the fish.

Big fish such

as shark, swordfish, and marlin take years to reach their size. Overfishing these large fish can have grave consequences. Furthermore, these fish higher up the food chain are also those most likely to have accumulated levels of mercury that may be damaging to our health. By choosing smaller fish you have a win-win on both fronts.

Soba noodles are a low-GI Japanese noodle made from a mixture of buckwheat and wheat, making them high in dietary fiber and a complete protein. Sodium content is high; however, this is reduced significantly after cooking.

thai shrimp with soba noodles and asparagus

6½ ounces green tea soba noodles

¾ pound thin asparagus, halved crosswise

½ cup shelled frozen edamame, thawed

1 cup fresh mint leaves

1 cup fresh Thai basil leaves

16 uncooked large shrimp, peeled, deveined, with tails intact

2 tablespoons olive oil

2 limes, cut into wedges

dressing

2 tablespoons finely grated palm sugar

⅓ cup lime juice

¼ cup fish sauce

2 fresh small red chiles, seeded, chopped finely

¼ cup peanut oil

1 Make dressing.

2 Cook noodles in a saucepan of boiling water for 2 minutes or until almost tender. Add asparagus; cook a further 2 minutes or until noodles and asparagus are just tender. Drain, refresh under cold water; drain.

3 Place noodles and asparagus in a large bowl with edamame, herbs, and dressing; toss gently to combine.

4 Combine shrimp and oil in a medium bowl. Cook shrimp on a heated grill pan (or under a broiler or on a grill) for 1½ minutes each side or until just cooked through.

5 Serve noodle salad topped with shrimp and lime wedges.

dressing Whisk ingredients together in a small bowl until sugar dissolves.

prep + cook time 25 minutes **serves** 4
nutritional count per serving 25.3g total fat (4.5g saturated fat); 481 cal; 22.1g carbohydrate; 22g protein; 6g fiber

tip Asparagus spears vary in thickness; if the ends are really thick, peel them from the bottom up to within 2 inches of the tips.

For a light lunch you could probably get away with one small portion of fish. For heartier eaters, or as a main meal, you will want the quantity here.

bream with kohlrabi, watercress, and walnut salad with buttermilk dressing

¾ pound kohlrabi, trimmed, unpeeled

6 cups watercress sprigs

½ cup coarsely chopped roasted walnuts

2 green onions (scallions), sliced thinly

8 x 4½-ounce bream fillets

2 tablespoons olive oil

buttermilk dressing

1 tablespoon Dijon mustard

1 tablespoon rice wine vinegar

¼ cup olive oil

⅓ cup buttermilk

⅓ cup fresh dill sprigs

1 Make Buttermilk Dressing.

2 Using a mandoline or V-slicer, slice kohlrabi into matchsticks (or grate coarsely). Place in a large bowl with watercress, nuts, onion, and dressing; toss gently to combine.

3 Season fish on both sides. Heat oil in a large frying pan over high heat; cook fish, in two batches, for 1 minute each side or until just cooked through. Cover fish with foil, between batches, to keep warm.

4 Serve fish with kohlrabi salad.

buttermilk dressing Place ingredients in a screw-top jar; shake well. Season to taste. Refrigerate until needed.

prep + cook time 30 minutes **serves** 4
nutritional count per serving 48.3g total fat (9.9g saturated fat); 731 cal; 6.7g carbohydrate; 65.8g protein; 4.9g fiber

Butterflied sardines are boneless with the two fillets attached. To do this yourself, cut off the head just behind the gills. With a small knife, cut along the belly, from head to tail, then open out. Holding the spine at head end, pull it down firmly towards the tail end and snip with scissors to release it.

grilled sardines with fennel and preserved lemon

2 teaspoons fennel seeds

½ teaspoon sea salt flakes

1 teaspoon freshly ground black pepper

12 butterflied sardines

⅓ cup olive oil

2 tablespoons finely chopped preserved lemon rind

2 tablespoons lemon juice

¼ pound baby green beans, trimmed

1 baby baby fennel, trimmed

1 small Persian cucumber

¼ pound radishes, sliced thinly

1 large avocado, sliced

1 Using a mortar and pestle, crush fennel seeds with salt and pepper. Place sardines on a tray; sprinkle seed mixture on both sides. Cover with plastic wrap; refrigerate 20 minutes.

2 Meanwhile, place ¼ cup olive oil, preserved lemon rind, and juice in a screw-top jar; shake well. Season to taste.

3 Cook beans in a saucepan of boiling salted water for 2 minutes or until just tender; drain. When cool enough to handle, cut beans in half lengthwise.

4 Using a mandoline or V-slicer, cut fennel into very thin slices. Using a vegetable peeler, peel cucumber into ribbons.

5 Place beans, fennel, cucumber, and radish in a large bowl with dressing; toss gently to combine.

6 Heat remaining oil in a large frying pan over medium-high heat; cook sardines for 1 minute each side or until just cooked through.

7 Layer salad and avocado on plates, top with sardines; serve immediately.

prep + cook time 35 minutes (+ refrigeration) serves 4
nutritional count per serving 41.5g total fat (8.4g saturated fat); 495 cal; 4.4g carbohydrate; 24.9g protein; 4.1g fiber

lean meats

Choosing the right meats can make a huge difference to your health and well-being, as well as that of the planet.

Sesame seeds contain a wonderful array of minerals. They are particularly rich in manganese and copper, and also provide significant levels of calcium, iron, magnesium, phosphorus, and zinc. Tahini, a sesame seed spread, is a great way to give your body a sesame nutritional boost.

korean steak tacos with pickled vegetables

2 x 8-ounce grass-fed beef porterhouse steaks

1½-inch piece fresh ginger, grated

2 cloves garlic, crushed, plus 1 clove garlic, sliced

2 tablespoons light soy sauce

½ teaspoon chile flakes

1 medium carrot, unpeeled, sliced thinly

1 Persian cucumber, sliced thinly

1 small red onion, sliced thinly

2 tablespoons rice wine vinegar

1 teaspoon caster (superfine) sugar

1 tablespoon vegetable oil

8 x 8-inch whole-grain tortillas

1 head butter (Boston) lettuce

¼ cup sweet chile sauce

2 teaspoons sesame seeds, toasted

½ cup loosely packed fresh cilantro leaves

1 Combine steaks, ginger, crushed garlic, sauce, and chile flakes in a large bowl. Cover; stand for 15 minutes.

2 Meanwhile, combine carrot, cucumber, onion, sliced garlic, vinegar, and sugar in a large bowl. Cover; let stand for 15 minutes.

3 Brush steaks on both sides with oil. Cook on heated grill pan (or grill) over high heat, for 2 minutes each side, for medium-rare or until cooked as desired. Remove from heat; cover with foil, let rest for 5 minutes.

4 Place tortillas on heated grill pan for 30 seconds each side or until charred lightly.

5 Cut steak into thin slices. Top each tortilla with a few small lettuce leaves, sliced steak, and pickled vegetables. Drizzle with chile sauce. Top with sesame seeds and cilantro.

prep + cook time 30 minutes (+ standing) **serves** 4
nutritional count per serving 27.8g total fat (9.3g saturated fat); 578 cal; 43.5g carbohydrate; 34g protein; 9g fiber

tip If tortillas are hard to separate, microwave in the opened bag for 30 seconds.

The low-fat dieting era popularized chicken fillets, because the dark chicken meat near the bone has more fat. However, chicken cooked on the bone is tastier and the dark meat contains more nutrients, particularly iron and zinc. To enjoy every cut of the chicken, guilt-free, ditch the extra calories in your diet by eliminating snack foods.

roast chicken with fava beans and lemon

1 medium lemon

3 cups fresh shelled fava beans

2 tablespoons olive oil

3 pounds chicken pieces, bone-in, skin-on

4 green onions (scallions), cut into 1½-inch lengths

4 cloves garlic, sliced thinly

8 sprigs fresh thyme

1½ cups chicken stock

2 tablespoons lemon juice

½ cup loosely packed fresh mint leaves

2 tablespoons capers, rinsed

1 Preheat oven to 400°F.

2 Using a vegetable peeler, peel four 2¾-inch strips of zest from the lemon. Squeeze juice from the lemon; you will need 2 tablespoons juice.

3 Cook fava beans in a saucepan of boiling water 2 minutes; drain. Refresh under cold running water; drain. Peel away skins then discard.

4 Heat oil in a large sauté pan over high heat; cook chicken pieces, in two batches, for 3 minutes each side or until browned. Remove from dish; drain excess fat from dish.

5 Add onion, garlic, thyme and zest strips to same dish; cook for 2 minutes. Return chicken and any juices to the dish with stock; bring to a boil. Transfer to the oven; cook, uncovered, for 40 minutes or until chicken is cooked through. Stir in fava beans; cook for a further 5 minutes or until heated through.

6 Serve chicken drizzled with lemon juice, topped with mint and capers.

prep + cook time 1 hour 15 minutes **serves** 4

nutritional count per serving 32.5g total fat (8.5g saturated fat); 521 cal; 5.9g carbohydrate; 47.3g protein; 9g fiber

tips You will need to buy about 3½ pounds fresh fava beans in the pod to yield 3 cups, or you can use frozen fava beans. You can cook baby potatoes with the chicken. If you prefer, you can use a 3-pound whole chicken chopped into pieces.

serving suggestion Serve with whole-wheat couscous.

Lamb is lean and healthy. High in protein and iron and low in fat, ground lamb is a great alternative to more popular red meats. It works particularly well as a substitute to ground beef in pasta dishes with meaty sauces.

Greek-style lamb bolognese

4 tablespoons olive oil

1 pound ground lamb

1 medium onion, chopped finely

4 cloves garlic, crushed

4 sprigs fresh oregano, plus ¼ cup loosely packed fresh oregano leaves

1 cup red wine

1½ pounds canned diced tomatoes

2 cups beef stock

1 teaspoon caster (superfine) sugar

12½ ounces whole-wheat spaghetti

⅓ cup pitted kalamata olives, sliced

4½ ounces Greek feta, crumbled

1 Heat 2 tablespoons oil in a large, heavy-based saucepan over high heat; cook ground lamb, onion, garlic, and oregano for 10 minutes or until browned, breaking up any lumps with a wooden spoon.
2 Add wine; cook for 1 minute. Add tomatoes, stock, and sugar; bring to a boil. Reduce heat to medium; cook for 30 minutes or until sauce has reduced and thickened. Season to taste.
3 Meanwhile, cook spaghetti in a large saucepan of boiling, salted water for 12 minutes or until almost tender. Drain.
4 Add spaghetti to sauce; toss to combine. Serve topped with olives, feta, and oregano leaves; drizzle with remaining oil.

prep + cook time 50 minutes **serves** 4
nutritional count per serving 33.7g total fat (9.9g saturated fat); 845 cal; 70.6g carbohydrate; 49.9g protein; 14.1g fiber

Quail is an excellent source of several of the B-group vitamins, especially niacin, with a single quail providing roughly half your daily requirement. Niacin plays a vital role in converting our food into energy and is essential for healthy skin and for nerves to function correctly.

grilled quail with cauliflower and pomegranate salad

1 small cauliflower, cut into ¾-inch florets

2 tablespoons olive oil

6 medium quails (2 pounds), butterflied (see tip)

2 teaspoons ground cilantro

1 teaspoon ground cinnamon

1 tablespoon fresh thyme leaves

2 tablespoons pomegranate molasses

2 Persian cucumbers, diced

1 medium red onion, chopped finely

4 green onions (scallions), sliced thinly

1⅓ cups chopped fresh flat-leaf parsley

½ cup chopped fresh mint

1 medium pomegranate, seeds removed

¼ cup lemon juice

¼ cup extra-virgin olive oil

½ teaspoon honey

1 Preheat oven 425°F.

2 Divide cauliflower between two large baking sheets; drizzle each tray with 2 teaspoons of the olive oil. Season. Bake for 15 minutes or until browned well.

3 Place quails on a large baking sheet, sprinkle with spices, drizzle with remaining olive oil; season. Cook quails, skin-side down first, on a heated grill pan (or grill) over medium-high heat, for 3 minutes each side or until browned. Return quails to baking sheet; top with thyme, drizzle with half the molasses. Bake for 8 minutes or until just cooked. Cover quail with foil; let rest for 5 minutes.

4 Meanwhile, place cauliflower in a large bowl with cucumber, onions, herbs, and half the pomegranate seeds. Whisk juice, extra-virgin olive oil, and honey in a small bowl. Pour dressing over salad; toss gently to combine.

5 Cut quails in half. Serve quail with cauliflower salad, drizzled with pan juices and remaining pomegranate molasses. Sprinkle with remaining pomegranate seeds.

prep + cook time 1 hour **serves** 4
nutritional count per serving 37.5g total fat (7.8g saturated fat); 645 cal; 23.6g carbohydrate; 47.3g protein; 13.2g fiber

tips To butterfly quails, cut down either side of the back bone with a pair of kitchen scissors, poultry shears, or a knife; discard backbone, open quails out flat. To remove seeds from the pomegranate, cut a whole pomegranate in half and scrape the seeds from flesh with your fingers while holding the pomegranate upside down in a bowl of cold water; the seeds will sink and the white pith will float.

TODAY

THE MEATS WE EAT THAT DOMINATE THE AMERICAN DIET ARE BEEF, LAMB, CHICKEN, AND PORK. DIVERSIFYING TO INCLUDE MORE GAME MEATS AND ALTERNATIVE POULTRY PROVIDES US WITH A NUTRITIONAL AND ENVIRONMENTAL BOOST.

Quail is produced in a free-range environment. The meat provides high biological value protein, is reasonably low in fat, and less than a third of that present is saturated fat. Quail is an excellent source of several of the B-group vitamins, especially niacin. A single quail provides roughly half your daily requirement. Niacin plays a vital role in converting our food into energy, and is essential for healthy skin and for nerves to function correctly.

quail & small chickens

From a sustainability and environmental perspective, there are advantages to our getting more of our protein from smaller, nonruminant animals. Game birds and poultry fit this bill. If we look back through time and consider the foods our ancestors ate, thus the foods that have fueled our evolution, smaller animals and birds would certainly have been hunted and been a regular part of our diet.

Small chickens

Spatchcock refers to a small, young chicken that has been prepared for easy cooking by removing the backbone to butterfly the bird. As with larger chickens, there is more iron and zinc in the leg and thigh meat of small chickens so be sure to eat all parts of the bird. You'll benefit from a boost of B-group vitamins, with niacin again a star player.

Quail is a good source of many minerals, including iron, zinc, selenium, phosphorus, and copper.

warm beef salad with black-eyed peas, corn, and chimichurri

You will need to start this recipe the day before as the black-eyed peas must be soaked overnight.

1 cup black-eyed peas

3 ears of corn, husks removed

2 tablespoons olive oil

3 x 6½-ounce sirloin steaks, trimmed

2 teaspoons ground cumin

2 teaspoons smoked paprika

1 medium red onion, halved, sliced thinly

½ pound heirloom tomatoes, halved

1 medium avocado, chopped

2 fresh long red chiles, sliced thinly

½ cup fresh cilantro leaves

2 tablespoons lime juice

2 tablespoons extra-virgin olive oil

chimichurri

2 cloves garlic, crushed

1 cup coarsely chopped fresh flat-leaf parsley leaves

½ cup coarsely chopped fresh cilantro leaves

1 teaspoon ground cumin

1 fresh small red chile, chopped finely

½ cup extra-virgin olive oil

3 teaspoons lime juice

1 Place black-eyed peas in a medium bowl of cold water; soak overnight.

2 Drain black-eyed peas. Cook peas in a large saucepan of boiling water for 15 minutes or until tender; drain. Rinse under cold water; drain well.

3 Meanwhile, make Chimichurri.

4 Brush corn with a little of the oil; season. Cook corn on a heated grill pan (or grill) over medium heat, turning occasionally, for 15 minutes or until charred and tender. Cool for 10 minutes. Cut kernels from ears of corn.

5 Brush steaks with a little of the oil, sprinkle with cumin and paprika; season. Cook steaks on heated grill plate over medium-high heat, for 3 minutes each side, depending on thickness, for medium-rare or until cooked as desired. Remove from pan; cover with foil, rest for 5 minutes.

6 Place peas and corn kernels in a large bowl with onion, tomatoes, avocado, chile, cilantro, juice, extra-virgin olive oil, and a third of the chimichurri, season; toss gently to combine.

7 Serve salad topped with sliced steak and drizzled with remaining chimichurri.

chimichurri Process garlic, herbs, cumin, chile, and 1 tablespoon of the oil until roughly chopped. With motor operating, add remaining oil in a thin steady stream until smooth. Stir in juice. Season to taste.

prep + cook time 1 hour 5 minutes (+ standing) **serves** 4
nutritional count per serving 94.8g total fat (21.4g saturated fat); 1292 cal; 39.2g carbohydrate; 60.2g protein; 29g fiber

tip Chimichurri is a traditional Argentinian herb sauce served with grilled meats.

venison with baby beet salad and raspberry vinaigrette

You can use beef tenderloin instead of the venison if you like.

12 baby red beets

12 baby golden beets

⅓ cup olive oil

2 pounds venison tenderloin

12 shallots

¼ pound baby spinach

⅓ cup sunflower seeds, roasted

2½ ounces raspberries

raspberry vinaigrette

⅓ cup raspberry vinegar

⅓ cup olive oil

1 clove garlic, crushed

¼ cup fresh tarragon leaves

¼ cup fresh mint leaves

¼ cup fresh flat-leaf parsley leaves

1 Preheat oven to 350°F.

2 Trim beets; reserve 3 ounces of the nicest, smallest beet leaves. Wash all beets well. Place in a roasting pan; drizzle with half the oil. Cover with foil; roast for 30 minutes or until tender. Stand for 10 minutes. When cool enough to handle, remove skins (the skins should slip off easily, if not use a small knife). Cut beets in half.

3 Meanwhile, tie venison with kitchen string at 1¼-inch intervals to form an even shape; season. Heat remaining oil over high heat in a large ovenproof frying pan; cook venison, turning, for 8 minutes or until browned all over. Add shallots; roast in the oven 20 minutes for medium-rare venison or until cooked as desired. Cover with foil; rest for 10 minutes. Cut venison into ½-inch slices.

4 Make Raspberry Vinaigrette.

5 Place beets and reserved beet leaves in a large bowl with spinach, seeds, and half the vinaigrette; toss to combine. Place salad on a platter; top with raspberries. Serve salad with venison; drizzle with remaining vinaigrette.

raspberry vinaigrette Place ingredients in a screw-top jar; shake well. Season to taste.

prep + cook time 1 hour **serves** 6
nutritional count per serving 33g total fat (5.7g saturated fat); 583 cal; 10g carbohydrate; 57.8g protein; 6.6g fiber

Turkey meat deserves to be embraced beyond festive eating, as it is a very rich source of protein in relation to calories; also all B vitamins are present in the meat, alongside iron and minerals. You can use ground chicken instead.

turkey koftas with fig and brown rice pilaf

You will need to soak 12 bamboo skewers in water for about 30 minutes before you start this recipe.

1 pound ground turkey

½ cup stale breadcrumbs

3 green onions (scallions), sliced thinly

2 cloves garlic, crushed

¼ teaspoon allspice

¼ teaspoon ground cilantro

¼ teaspoon ground chile

2 tablespoons olive oil

fig and brown rice pilaf

2 tablespoons olive oil

1 small onion, chopped finely

2 cloves garlic, crushed

1 tablespoon finely grated orange zest

1 teaspoon ground cinnamon

½ teaspoon ground cumin

½ teaspoon ground cilantro

1 pound packaged pre-cooked brown basmati rice

1 cup chicken stock

⅓ cup chopped dried figs

¼ pound baby spinach leaves

1 Combine turkey, breadcrumbs, onion, garlic, and spices in a large bowl. Roll 2 tablespoons of mixture into long oval shapes; you should have 12. Place koftas on a baking-paper-lined baking sheet; refrigerate for 1 hour.

2 Make Fig and Brown Rice Pilaf.

3 Meanwhile, insert a skewer into each kofta; brush kofta well with oil. Cook kofta on heated grill pan (or grill) on medium-high heat, turning occasionally, for 8 minutes or until cooked through.

4 Serve kofta with pilaf.

fig and brown rice pilaf Heat oil in a large saucepan over medium-high heat; cook onion and garlic, for 3 minutes or until soft. Stir in zest and spices; cook for 2 minutes. Add rice; stir to coat. Add stock; bring to a boil. Reduce heat to medium; cook, covered, for 8 minutes. Remove from heat; stir in figs and spinach. Season to taste.

prep + cook time 1 hour 20 minutes (+ refrigeration)
serves 4
nutritional count per serving 24.6g total fat (4.4g saturated fat); 604 cal; 57.9g carbohydrate; 34.2g protein; 6.9g fiber

serving suggestion Serve with yogurt.

RED MEAT IS a fabulous source of high quality protein. Research has pretty conclusively shown that high protein diets help us to control our weight and most importantly keep any lost weight off. If you've been on the dieting merry-go-round think about how much red meat you consume. You might just find that including a little more helps you to control your appetite and as a result, eat less. (Note that doesn't mean low carb —you can achieve a high-protein diet while eating a moderate amount of quality carbs. In fact, that is most likely to give you long-term success.)

OUR SUPERFOODS ARE LEAN RED MEATS THAT ARE WILD OR PASTURE/GRASS FED WHERE POSSIBLE. THEY ARE INCREDIBLY AND NATURALLY LEAN, WHILE BEING RICH IN NUTRIENTS AND A SOURCE OF OMEGA-3s. YOU MIGHT ALSO LIKE TO TRY VENISON IF YOU SPOT IT, BUT GRASS-FED BEEF AND LAMB ARE MOST WIDELY AVAILABLE AND WARRANT SUPERFOOD STATUS.

lean red meat

We can live without meat and we have every respect for those who are vegetarian... but there is no denying the nutritional benefits of good quality red meat. One of the most common nutrient deficiencies in the developed world is iron deficiency. In the extreme it results in anemia, but even mild deficiencies cause an intolerance to cold, depressed immune function so more frequent coughs and colds, and an inability to exercise at your best. The trouble is, we're not very good at absorbing iron, particularly from plants. That's where red meat comes in. The heme iron in meat is far better absorbed. Unfortunately it is women who need more iron, yet are the ones most likely to cut down on red meat.

If you're worried about the press there has been surrounding meat and colon cancer, be assured that the strongest evidence is for processed meats such as ham, bacon, salami, and sausages. Fresh lean red meat is a different prospect. Grass-fed meat is the best quality. It has higher levels of beneficial fats such as the omega-3s and lower overall levels of fat, especially long-chain saturated fats.

RED MEAT is also rich in another mineral often low in typical diets—zinc. This is essential for immune function, hence you'll find it added to cold and flu remedies. Eating red meat a few times a week is all you need to significantly zinc-boost your diet.

white cooked chicken with ginger rice

2¾-pound whole chicken

3 green onions (scallions), sliced finely

2½-inch piece fresh ginger, cut into matchsticks

2 teaspoons sesame oil

2½ teaspoons caster (superfine) sugar

2 tablespoons peanut oil

¼ cup light soy sauce

2 tablespoons oyster sauce

¾ gai lan, trimmed, chopped

1 fresh long red chile, sliced thinly

white master stock

20 cups cold water

2½ cups Chinese rice wine (shao hsing)

8 green onions (scallions), trimmed, halved

10 cloves garlic, bruised

5½ ounces fresh ginger, sliced

2 tablespoons salt

ginger rice

2 cups jasmine rice

1 tablespoon vegetable oil

1 clove garlic, crushed

4-inch piece fresh ginger, sliced thinly

1 Make White Master Stock.

2 Remove excess fat from chicken cavity, then rinse chicken. Carefully lower chicken, breast-side down, into simmering master stock, ensuring it is fully submerged. Poach chicken 30 minutes (there should be no more than the occasional ripple). Remove pan from heat; leave chicken in poaching liquid for 3 hours at room temperature to complete the cooking process. Using tongs, gently remove chicken from stock, being careful not to tear the breast. Place chicken on a tray; cool. Strain poaching liquid through a fine sieve; reserve poaching liquid.

3 Make Ginger Rice.

4 Place onion, ginger, half the sesame oil, ½ teaspoon of the sugar, and 2 tablespoons of the reserved poaching liquid in a bowl. Heat peanut oil in a small frying pan until hot. Taking care, as mixture will split, pour hot oil over ginger mixture; reserve until ready to serve.

5 Place sauces, remaining sesame oil and remaining sugar in a screw-top jar; shake well. Cook gai lan in a large saucepan of boiling water for 2 minutes or until just tender; drain. Transfer gai lan to a serving bowl; add dressing and top with chile.

6 Chop chicken into pieces and arrange on a platter; pour over reserved ginger mixture. Serve with ginger rice and gai lan.

white master stock Place ingredients in a large saucepan; bring to a boil. Reduce heat; simmer gently for 40 minutes.

ginger rice Rinse rice in a sieve under cold water until water runs clear. Heat oil in a large saucepan over medium heat; cook garlic and ginger 3 minutes. Add rice and 1 quart of the reserved poaching liquid; bring to a boil. Reduce heat to low; cook, covered, for 10 minutes or until most liquid is absorbed. Remove from heat; let stand, covered, 10 minutes.

prep + cook time 4 hours 30 minutes
serves 6 as part of a banquet
nutritional count per serving 25.2g total fat (6.1g saturated fat); 701 cal; 63.5g carbohydrate; 31.9g protein; 3.3g fiber

sumac chile lamb

1 large red onion, cut into wedges

2 medium red bell peppers, cut into strips

¾ pound small carrots, trimmed, unpeeled

3 finger eggplants, sliced lengthwise

¼ cup plus 1 tablespoon olive oil

1¾ pounds lamb backstraps, trimmed

2 tablespoons sumac

1 teaspoon dried chile flakes

3 ounces baby arugula

¼ cup lemon juice

2 tablespoons extra-virgin olive oil

white bean puree

1½ pounds canned cannellini beans, drained, rinsed

1 clove garlic, crushed

¼ cup lemon juice

⅓ cup olive oil

1 Preheat oven to 350°F. Line a large baking sheet with parchment paper.

2 Place vegetables on baking sheet, drizzle with ¼ cup olive oil and season; toss to combine. Roast for 30 minutes or until tender.

3 Meanwhile, rub lamb with 1 tablespoon olive oil then roll in sumac and chile. Cook lamb on heated grill pan (or grill) over medium-high heat, turning occasionally, for 4 minutes, for medium-rare or until cooked to your liking. Cover with foil; let rest for 5 minutes.

4 Meanwhile, make White Bean Puree.

5 Add arugula to vegetables, drizzle with juice and extra-virgin olive oil; toss to combine. Spoon half the bean puree among plates, top with vegetable mixture. Cut lamb into thin slices; place on salad, drizzle with remaining bean puree.

white bean puree Process ingredients until smooth, adding a little water if necessary, until mixture reaches a dipping consistency. Season to taste.

prep + cook time 45 minutes **serves** 4
nutritional count per serving 63.3g total fat (12.2g saturated fat); 934 cal; 25.6g carbohydrate; 60g protein; 13.8g fiber

Although pork is perceived as being a fatty meat, a trimmed fillet is only about 2% fat. Pork breeding has changed in recent years making most pork these days pretty lean.

five-spice pork fillet

2 shallots, sliced thinly

2 cloves garlic, sliced thinly

4 pears, each cut into 6 wedges

1½-inch piece ginger, cut into matchsticks

2 tablespoons brown sugar

2 tablespoons soy sauce

2 teaspoons Chinese five-spice powder

¼ cup olive oil

1½ pounds pork fillet, trimmed

2 tablespoons sesame seeds

3 ounces yellow beans

3 ounces baby green beans

1 Preheat oven to 350°F. Line a roasting pan with parchment paper.

2 Place shallots, garlic, pears, ginger, sugar, sauce, and five-spice in the pan, drizzle with 2 tablespoons of the oil; toss to combine. Roast for 20 minutes or until pears are just soft.

3 Meanwhile, rub pork with 2 teaspoons of the oil; roll in seeds. Heat remaining oil in an ovenproof frying pan over medium heat; cook pork until brown on all sides. Transfer pan to oven; roast pork for 12 minutes or just cooked through. Cover pork with foil; rest for 5 minutes.

4 Meanwhile, boil, steam, or microwave beans for 3 minutes or until just tender; drain.

5 Serve sliced pork with roasted pear mixture, sauce, and beans.

prep + cook time 40 minutes **serves** 4
nutritional count per serving 21.5g total fat (4.3g saturated fat); 489 cal; 19.6g carbohydrate; 47.3g protein; 8.2g fiber

Pork is STRICTLY SPEAKING A RED MEAT; HOWEVER, NUTRITIONALLY ITS PROFILE IS CLOSER TO WHITE MEAT. ALTHOUGH IT IS PERCEIVED AS BEING A FATTY MEAT, PORK BREEDING HAS CHANGED IN RECENT YEARS AND IN FACT MOST PORK TODAY IS PRETTY LEAN. AS WITH BIRDS, THE FAT IS SEPARABLE AND SO, ONCE TRIMMED, PORK IS ONE OF THE LEANEST MEATS. A TRIMMED PORK FILLET IS ONLY ABOUT 2% FAT. PORK IS ALSO EXCEPTIONALLY RICH IN THIAMIN (VITAMIN B1), AND 3 OUNCES OF RAW PORK FILLET, WHEN COOKED, PROVIDES 75% OF YOUR DAILY REQUIREMENT.

Pork is exceptionally rich in thiamin. Thiamin plays an essential role in metabolism, particularly of carbohydrates. Your requirement for thiamin is also increased if you drink alcohol.

white meats

White meats are essentially chicken and turkey, along with less commonly eaten birds and poultry. Nutritionally, these meats tend to be lower in calories and fat than red meats, although there are exceptions. However, even in those birds with higher fat levels such as duck and goose, the fat is almost all in and just under the skin. This means that, unlike marbled fatty meats, you can remove most of the fat if you wish.

You don't really need to be so concerned about the fat on birds and poultry. The old days of trying to avoid all fat are long gone. We now know that it is processed fats in packaged foods and fast food that are most detrimental to us.

Some saturated fats are also known to worsen blood cholesterol profiles, may be harder to burn as fuel in the body, and can have other negative effects at a cellular level. Monounsaturated fats, like those found in avocado and olive oil, seem to help reduce fat around your middle, be more readily burned as fuel, and may also reduce the risk of several chronic diseases. Poultry, duck, and other birds have a high percentage of these monounsaturated fats, making them a healthier choice than fatty red meat cuts.

coconut–cilantro chicken and vegetable curry

4 fresh long green chiles

1 large onion, chopped

2-inch piece fresh ginger, chopped

4 cloves garlic, chopped

1 tablespoon ground cilantro

1 tablespoon ground cumin

1 teaspoon salt

2 pounds chicken thigh fillets

9 fluid ounces canned coconut milk

2 cups chicken stock

1¼ pounds orange sweet potato, unpeeled, cut into 1-inch pieces

½ pound cauliflower, chopped

3 ounces baby spinach

1 tablespoon sesame seeds

⅓ cup roasted salted cashews

1 cup Greek-style yogurt

½ cup coarsely chopped cilantro leaves, plus ¼ cup lightly packed fresh cilantro sprigs

¼ cup coarsely chopped fresh mint leaves

1 lime, cut into wedges

1 Remove seeds from two of the chiles; chop seeded chiles and one whole chile.

2 To make curry paste, blend chopped chile, onion, ginger, garlic, spices, and salt until smooth.

3 Trim fat from chicken; cut chicken into 1½-inch pieces. Heat 2 tablespoons of the coconut milk in a large saucepan over medium heat, add curry paste; cook, stirring, 3 minutes or until fragrant. Add chicken; cook, stirring, for 2 minutes or until combined. Add stock and remaining coconut milk; bring to a boil. Reduce heat; simmer, covered, for 10 minutes.

4 Add sweet potato to curry; simmer, covered, 5 minutes. Add cauliflower; simmer, covered, a further 5 minutes or until sweet potato and cauliflower are just tender. Stir in spinach until wilted.

5 Meanwhile, dry-fry seeds and nuts until browned lightly. Remove from pan; cool. Blend nut mixture until ground finely. Stir nut mixture into curry; stir in ¾ cup of the yogurt and the chopped herbs. Season to taste.

6 Serve curry drizzled with remaining yogurt, topped with remaining chile, chopped, and cilantro sprigs. Serve with lime wedges.

prep + cook time 50 minutes **serves** 6
nutritional count per serving 49g total fat (20g saturated fat); 720 cal; 30.8g carbohydrate; 36.2g protein; 7.4g fiber

tip Long chiles are usually mild but can vary in their heat intensity. Adjust the amount of chiles you use (or remove the seeds and membranes from all of them), according to your tolerance level.

serving suggestion Serve with steamed basmati or brown rice.

pork and fennel ragù with sweet potato and goat cheese gnocchi

3¼-pound piece boneless pork shoulder

2 tablespoons spelt flour

1 tablespoon extra-virgin olive oil

2 medium leeks, white part only, sliced

2 trimmed celery stalks, chopped

2 medium fennel bulbs, fronds reserved, sliced thinly

4 cloves garlic, chopped

1 teaspoon chopped fresh thyme leaves

¼ teaspoon dried chile flakes

2 cups chicken stock

1 cup water

1 cup whole marinated green Sicilian olives

1 tablespoon lemon juice

sweet potato and goat cheese gnocchi

2 pounds orange sweet potato, unpeeled

¼ pound soft goat cheese, crumbled

2 egg yolks

1 cup spelt flour, approximately

1 Remove zest and trim fat from pork. Cut pork into six pieces, toss in flour; shake away excess. Heat oil in a casserole dish over high heat; cook pork, in batches, for 10 minutes or until browned lightly. Remove from dish.

2 Cook leek, celery, and fennel in same dish, stirring, over medium heat for 8 minutes or until softened. Add garlic, thyme, and chile; cook, stirring, 1 minute or until fragrant. Add stock and water; bring to a boil. Return pork to pan; stir to cover with liquid. Reduce heat to very low; simmer, covered, for 2 hours or until tender, stirring occasionally.

3 Meanwhile, make Sweet Potato and Goat Cheese Gnocchi.

4 Remove pork from pan; shred into smaller chunks. Return pork to pan with olives and juice. Season to taste. Cover; keep warm over low heat.

5 Cook gnocchi, in batches, in a large saucepan of boiling salted water for 2 minutes or until gnocchi float to the surface. Remove gnocchi with a slotted spoon; drain on paper towel.

6 Serve gnocchi topped with ragù, sprinkled with reserved fennel fronds and extra thyme leaves, if you like.

sweet potato and goat cheese gnocchi Place whole sweet potato in a medium saucepan; cover with cold water. Cover; bring to a boil. Reduce heat; simmer, partially covered, for 45 minutes or until tender. Drain. Cool slightly; peel. Mash sweet potato in a large bowl until smooth. Cool to room temperature. Stir in cheese and egg yolks; season. Add enough of the flour to mix to a soft, slightly sticky dough. Divide mixture into six portions; roll each portion on a floured surface into a ¾-inch thick log. Using a floured knife, cut logs into ¾-inch lengths. Place gnocchi on a large plastic-wrap-lined tray in a single layer. Cover; refrigerate until required.

prep + cook time 2 hours 50 minutes **serves** 6
nutritional count per serving 12.7g total fat (4.8g saturated fat); 597 cal; 57.9g carbohydrate; 57.9g protein; 8.8g fiber

tips Prepare the ragù several hours or a day ahead; refrigerate until cold, then skim any fat from the surface before reheating. You can use feta instead of goat cheese.

lamb wraps with
red salad and harissa yogurt

1 pound lamb backstraps

2 tablespoons harissa

2 tablespoons extra-virgin olive oil

4 whole-grain barley wraps

¼ small red cabbage, shredded finely

1 medium beet, grated coarsely

½ medium red onion, sliced thinly

4 radishes, sliced thinly

1 tablespoon lemon juice

1 clove garlic, crushed

⅔ cup Greek-style yogurt

⅓ cup loosely packed fresh cilantro sprigs

⅓ cup loosely packed fresh mint sprigs

1 Preheat oven to 350°F.

2 Rub lamb with half the harissa; drizzle with half the oil. Season. Cook lamb on heated grill pan (or under the broiler or on a grill) over medium-low heat, covered with a sheet of foil, for 4 minutes each side for medium or until done as desired. Remove lamb from heat; cover with foil, rest for 5 minutes.

3 Meanwhile, enclose barley wraps in foil; heat in oven 5 minutes.

4 For red salad, place cabbage, beet, onion, and radish in a large bowl with juice, garlic, and remaining oil; toss gently to combine. Season to taste.

5 Swirl remaining harissa through yogurt.

6 Slice lamb thinly. Divide lamb, red salad, yogurt mixture and herbs among wraps; roll up to serve.

prep + cook time 30 minutes **serves** 4
nutritional count per serving 21.5g total fat (6g saturated fat); 493 cal; 35.2g carbohydrate; 35.8g protein; 6.9g fiber

tip We used a milder harissa rather than the much hotter Tunisian one available in a tube. If using harissa in a tube, start with 1 teaspoon and add more to taste.

steak with cashew nam jim and asian greens

1½ pounds thick-cut rump steak

1 tablespoon peanut oil

¾ pound gai lan

½ pound baby bok choy, trimmed, quartered

3 ounces snow peas

4 green onions (scallions), sliced thinly

¼ cup unsalted roasted cashews, chopped coarsely

¼ cup loosely packed fresh cilantro sprigs

cashew nam jim

2 shallots, chopped

2 cloves garlic

3 fresh long green chiles, seeded, chopped

2 fresh cilantro roots, chopped

¾-inch piece fresh ginger, chopped

2 tablespoons grated dark palm sugar

⅓ cup unsalted roasted cashews

⅓ cup lime juice, approximately

1 tablespoon fish sauce, approximately

1 Make Cashew Nam Jim.

2 Trim fat from steak; rub with oil, season. Cook steak on a heated grill pan (or under the broiler or on a grill) on medium-high heat for 4 minutes each side for medium, or until done as desired. Remove steak from heat; cover with foil, rest for 5 minutes.

3 Meanwhile, trim gai lan stalks; cut stalks from leaves. Steam stalks, in a single layer, in a large steamer over a wok or large suacepan of boiling water for 1 minute. Place separated bok choy on top; steam a further 2 minutes. Add snow peas and gai lan leaves; steam a further 2 minutes or until vegetables are just tender.

4 Place vegetables on a platter in layers, top with thickly sliced steak. Drizzle with steak resting juices, then top with cashew nam jim. Sprinkle with onion, nuts, and cilantro.

cashew nam jim Blend shallots, garlic, chile, cilantro root, ginger, sugar, and cashews (or pound with a mortar and pestle) until mixture forms a paste. Transfer to a small bowl; stir in juice and fish sauce to taste.

prep + cook time 40 minutes serves 4
nutritional count per serving 35g total fat (9.7g saturated fat); 670 cal; 14g carbohydrate; 76.4g protein; 7.4g fiber

tips You will need about 3 limes for this recipe. Nam jim can be made a day ahead; keep tightly covered in the fridge until ready to use.

serving suggestion Serve with steamed jasmine or brown rice.

fruit & chocolate

We have an innate love of sweetness that is easy to exploit. But choose the right treats and you can not only enjoy them, you can give your health a boost at the same time.

Cherries are rich in vitamins and minerals as well as antioxidants. While fresh is best, if they are out of season, you can use frozen pitted cherries in this recipe instead.

apple, cherry, and rosemary crumble

8 medium red apples

¼ cup water

3 cups cherries, pitted

1 teaspoon ground cinnamon

2 teaspoons vanilla extract

⅓ cup plus 2 tablespoons pure maple syrup

1½ cups almonds

1 cup whole-wheat self-rising flour

3 teaspoons fresh rosemary leaves, chopped finely

½ cup coconut oil, melted

1½ cups unsweetened vanilla-bean yogurt

1 Preheat oven to 350°F.

2 Peel and core apples; cut into ¾-inch pieces. Place apples and the water in a large saucepan; bring to a boil. Reduce heat to low; cook, covered, for 10 minutes or until apples are just tender.

3 Place apples and cooking liquid in a large bowl; stir in cherries, cinnamon, extract, and ⅓ cup maple syrup until combined. Spoon into a 2-quart shallow ovenproof dish.

4 Process nuts, flour, and rosemary until nuts are chopped coarsely. With motor operating, add coconut oil and remaining maple syrup until well combined. Spoon crumble mixture over fruit (piling crumble high on top of fruit as it will sink down during cooking).

5 Bake for 40 minutes or until crumble topping is golden and fruit is soft. Serve with yogurt.

prep + cook time 1 hour **serves** 6
nutritional count per serving 45g total fat (21.5g saturated fat); 757 cal; 68.5g carbohydrate; 15.6g protein; 10.7g fiber

tip Coconut oil is a solidified oil sold in jars and is available from supermarkets and health food stores. Melt coconut oil as you would butter, either in a small saucepan over low heat or in the microwave.

The winter months are citrus heaven for cooks. Swap navel oranges for tangy tangelos (a cross between grapefruit and mandarin), large perfumed mandarins, or ruby red grapefruit, or a mix of all of them.

orange and lemon yogurt cups

1 vanilla bean

⅓ cup low-GI caster (superfine) sugar (see tips)

½ cup water

4 wide strips lemon zest

1 tablespoon lemon juice

2 blood oranges, zest removed, sliced

2 medium oranges, zest removed, sliced

3 cups Greek-style yogurt

¼ cup loosely packed fresh mint leaves

1 Split vanilla bean in half lengthwise; scrape seeds into a small saucepan. Add vanilla bean to pan with sugar, the water and zest; bring to a boil. Reduce heat; simmer for 6 minutes or until syrup has thickened slightly. Cool. Discard vanilla bean; stir in juice.

2 Combine orange slices and sugar syrup in a medium bowl.

3 Spoon yogurt into four 1¼ cup serving glasses; top with oranges, syrup, and zest. Serve topped with mint.

prep + cook time 45 minutes **serves** 4

nutritional count per serving 12.7g total fat (8g saturated fat); 419 cal; 59.7g carbohydrate; 12.4g protein; 4.5g fiber

tips You can also use coconut sugar or agave for this recipe. For lemon strips, use a vegetable peeler to peel wide strips and avoid taking off too much of the white pith with the zest as it is bitter. The syrup can be made 4 hours ahead and combined with the oranges; refrigerate until needed.

COCOA BEANS ARE FERMENTED, DRIED, AND ROASTED, AND THE SHELL REMOVED TO PRODUCE CACAO NIBS. THESE ARE THEN GROUND AND THIS FORMS THE BASIS OF CHOCOLATE. USUALLY THE CACAO IS SEPARATED TO GIVE COCOA BUTTER AND COCOA SOLIDS, AND YOU'LL FIND THESE LISTED AS INGREDIENTS ON THE PACK. SINCE THIS IS STILL A VERY BITTER TASTE, MOST CHOCOLATE IS SWEETENED AND MAY HAVE OTHER INGREDIENTS ADDED.

It's not just

your imagination. Chocolate really can cheer you up! The carbohydrates present raise levels of serotonin, the feel-good chemical in your brain, and chocolate contains a natural chemical called phenylethylamine that acts as a mood elevator.

Good quality

chocolate is not cholesterol raising and may even help to improve your overall cholesterol profile. Although cocoa butter is high in saturated fat, the main saturated fat present is stearic acid. This fat does not raise LDL cholesterol, the so-called bad cholesterol. In fact studies have associated stearic acid with lower LDL cholesterol. A good percentage of the other fats present are healthy monounsaturated fats, including oleic acid, the main fat in olive oil.

chocolate & cocoa

Several of the foods of ancient populations such as the Incas, Aztecs, and Mayans are considered superfoods today, and cocoa is one of them. Of course they didn't eat chocolate as we know it today, but they took the cacao bean and made it into a bitter tasting chocolate drink. Today chocolate is made far more delectable, but that also makes it easier to overeat.

Chocolate is energy-

dense, meaning each bite contains a significant number of calories. Devouring blocks of chocolate every day will clearly not help your waistline. You're better off opting for dark chocolate with as high a cocoa content as possible (or that you can enjoy). This means you get the maximal amount of cocoa for antioxidant benefits, while limiting added sugar, and the rich taste will mean you are satisfied with a small amount. Think quality over quantity.

One of the best ways to enjoy cocoa is by using pure cocoa powder (not to be confused with drinking chocolate powder). This ranks exceptionally high for antioxidant power, it's unexpectedly high in fiber, a good source of protein, and has no added sugar or other undesirable additives. It also provides significant amounts of iron, magnesium, phosphorus, manganese, and copper. You can add a tablespoon to milk along with a pinch of cinnamon and heat through to make a delicious chocolatey drink, or use in cooking and baking.

Unlike most chocolate mousse recipes, this one can be served the minute it is made. If you do wish to make it a day ahead, refrigerate, covered, then bring to room temperature before serving. You could also top each serving with cherries.

dark chocolate and ricotta mousse

⅓ cup brown rice syrup

1 tablespoon dutch-processed cocoa

2 tablespoons water

½ teaspoon vanilla extract

6½ ounces dark chocolate (70% cocoa), chopped

8 fresh dates, pitted

½ cup milk

2 cups ricotta

2 tablespoons pomegranate seeds

2 tablespoon chopped pistachios

1 Stir syrup, cocoa, the water, and extract in a small saucepan over medium heat; bring to a boil. Remove from heat; cool.
2 Place chocolate in a small heatproof bowl over a small saucepan of simmering water (don't let the water touch the base of the bowl); stir until melted and smooth.
3 Process dates and milk until dates are finely chopped. Add ricotta; process until smooth. Add melted chocolate; process until well combined.
4 Spoon mousse into six ¾ cup serving glasses. Spoon cocoa syrup on mousse; top with pomegranate seeds and nuts.

prep + cook time 20 minutes **serves** 6
nutritional count per serving 21g total fat (12g saturated fat); 482 cal; 62g carbohydrate; 12.3g protein; 3.8g fiber

tips Fresh pomegranate seeds can sometimes be found in the fridge section of supermarkets or good green grocers. If unavailable, cut a whole pomegranate in half and scrape the seeds from the flesh with your fingers while holding the pomegranate upside down in a bowl of cold water; the seeds will sink and the white pith will float. Pomegranate seeds will keep refrigerated for up to a week.

One point to

note is that carotenoids, including beta-cryptoxanthin, are fat-soluble and therefore you need to have fat present to absorb them. You might like to ensure you eat some citrus at the end of a meal containing healthy fats, snack on themalongside a handful of nuts, or add them to salad with an extra-virgin olive oil–based dressing to get the full benefit.

TANGERINES AND ORANGES ARE ONE OF THE RICHEST DIETARY SOURCES OF ONE OF THE CAROTENOID ANTIOXIDANTS CALLED BETA-CRYPTOXANTHIN. SOME RESEARCH STUDIES HAVE SHOWN THIS TO REDUCE THE RISK OF LUNG AND COLON CANCERS, AND IT MAY ALSO REDUCE THE RISK OF INFLAMMATORY DISORDERS SUCH AS RHEUMATOID ARTHRITIS.

CITRUS FRUITS

include oranges, tangerines, mandarins, grapefruit varieties, clementine, kumquats, lemons, and limes.

citrus

They are most famous for their vitamin C content—a single orange provides you with about 1.5 times your daily requirement. A good body of research suggests that optimal levels of vitamin C are somewhat higher than currently recommended. As a water-soluble nutrient, we cannot store it in the body and therefore need a vitamin C source in our diet every day for optimal health.

Grapefruit is rich in a flavonoid antioxidant called naringin. This plays a role in protecting the lungs from cellular damage caused by pollutants in the air and from cigarette smoke. Vitamin C is also important here, making grapefruit a particularly good superfood for lung health. Naringin may also be involved in lowering the risk of colon cancer. Pink and red grapefruits get their color from the carotenoids present, which may offer additional antioxidant benefits.

Try where

possible to eat some citrus fruit skin. It contains two antioxidants, limonene and coumarin, which have been shown to stimulate a detoxification enzyme that in turn helps rid the body of potentially carcinogenic compounds. Try adding some grated zest to your food, or gently stew lesser known citrus fruits such as kumquats, where you can, then eat the whole fruit, including the skin.

There are two types of persimmons available in the cooler months: astringent and non-astringent. The first, hachiya, is heart shaped and is eaten very ripe, otherwise the taste is very astringent. The other, which is sometimes called fuyu, is squat and eaten crisp.

honey and lime baked persimmons

You can use either type of persimmon in this recipe. If you use the astringent variety, it is best to scrape away the flesh from the skin when eating.

4 persimmons (2 pounds), each cut into 6 wedges

1 lime, sliced thinly

1½-inch piece fresh ginger, sliced thinly

1½ tablespoons honey

6½ ounces passionfruit frozen yogurt

1 tablespoon lime zest strips

1 Preheat oven to 400°F. Cut four 14-inch pieces of parchment paper.
2 Place pieces of paper lengthwise in front of you, then divide persimmon wedges among parchment paper, placing them crosswise in the center. Top with lime slices and ginger; drizzle with honey. Bring short edges of paper together, fold over several times to secure, then tuck sides under to form a parcel. Place parcels on two baking sheets.
3 Bake parcels for 15 minutes or until persimmon is soft. Serve opened parcels topped with spoonfuls of frozen yogurt and lime zest.

prep + cook time 25 minutes **serves** 4
nutritional count per serving 3g total fat (1.7g saturated fat); 286 cal; 58g carbohydrate; 4g protein; 7.4g fiber

tip Use a zester to make the lime zest strips. If you don't have one, finely grate the zest instead.

spelt crêpes with poached pears and blueberries

2 eggs

1 cup milk

⅓ cup plain (all-purpose) spelt flour

⅓ cup whole-grain spelt flour

11½ ounces ricotta

2 tablespoons pure maple syrup

1 teaspoon ground cinnamon

2 teaspoons coconut oil

poached pears and blueberries

½ cup red wine

½ cup freshly squeezed orange juice

1 cinnamon stick

2 tablespoons pure maple syrup

2 small pears, unpeeled

4 ounces blueberries

1 Make Poached Pears and Blueberries.

2 Meanwhile, process eggs, milk, and flours until smooth. Transfer to a bowl; let stand for 20 minutes.

3 Whisk ricotta, maple syrup and cinnamon in a small bowl until smooth.

4 Brush a heated 8-inch crêpe pan with a little of the coconut oil. Pour scant ¼ cups of batter into pan, swirling to coat the base; cook 30 seconds or until browned underneath. Turn crêpe; cook further 10 seconds or until browned lightly underneath. Transfer to a plate; cover to keep warm. Repeat with remaining oil and batter to make 8 crêpes in total.

5 Spread 2 tablespoons of the ricotta mixture on one quarter of each crêpe; fold crêpe into quarters over the filling. Serve crêpes with poached fruit and poaching liquid.

poached pears and blueberries Bring wine, juice, cinnamon, and syrup to a boil in a medium saucepan over medium heat. Meanwhile, quarter and core pears; cut into thin wedges. Add pear wedges to wine mixture; simmer, uncovered, 10 minutes or until tender. Add blueberries; remove from heat.

prep + cook time 35 minutes (+ standing) **serves** 4
nutritional count per serving 15g total fat (9g saturated fat); 438 cal; 52g carbohydrate; 17g protein; 6.8g fiber

tips The cooking time of the pear wedges will depend on the ripeness. Buy ricotta fresh from the deli; it should be moist.

Buy fresh ricotta cut from a wheel from a deli or the deli counter of a supermarket for the best texture. Pre-packaged ricotta will be too wet for this recipe. Cooling the cheesecake in the oven after it has been turned off ensures that it will cool slowly and prevent the top from cracking.

ricotta and chocolate cheesecake with grapes

1 vanilla bean

1½ pounds ricotta

½ cup plus 1 tablespoon honey

2 tablespoons caster (superfine) sugar

2 teaspoons finely grated orange zest

3 eggs

4½ ounces dark chocolate (70% cocoa), chopped finely

1 cup small red grapes, plus ¼ pound little bunches red grapes

1 Preheat the oven to 300°F. Grease a 9-inch springform pan; line base and side with parchment paper, extending the paper 1¼ inches above the edge.
2 Split vanilla bean in half lengthwise; scrape seeds into a large bowl of an electric mixer. Add ricotta, ½ cup honey, sugar, and zest to bowl; beat with an electric mixer on medium-high speed for 3 minutes or until smooth. Beat in eggs, one at time, until just combined. Stir in chocolate and ½ cup grapes. Pour mixture into pan; top with remaining ½ cup grapes.
3 Bake cheesecake for 55 minutes or until the center is almost firm to touch. Cool in the oven with the door ajar. Refrigerate cheesecake for 4 hours or until firm.
4 Just before serving, top cheesecake with the grape bunches; drizzle with extra honey.

prep + cook time 1 hour 30 minutes (+ cooling & refrigeration)
serves 12
nutritional count per serving 10g total fat (5.7g saturated fat); 237 cal; 30.4g carbohydrate; 7.8g protein; 0.4g fiber

tip When chopping the chocolate aim for fairly even pieces about ¼ inch in size.

Berries are high in vitamin C and contain many potentially beneficial plant chemicals that have been shown to have anti-cancer, anti-viral and anti-bacterial properties.

Pomegranate is an ancient fruit that remains popular in Mediterranean, Middle-Eastern, and Indian diets. In these areas pomegranate has long been used medicinally, but recent research is uncovering many factors about the fruit that may well account for some very real health benefits. Pomegranate is one of the highest ranking fruits for antioxidant power and it is particularly rich in a group of polyphenols called ellagitannins. This can bind cancer-causing molecules, rendering them inactive, and has been shown to have an anti-cancer effect on several cancers including breast, skin, prostate, and colon.

berries

The beautiful array of blues, reds, and purples of berries is indicative of the antioxidants present. The color comes from the anthocyanins present. These are part of the flavonoid family of antioxidants. Studies show a high intake of anthocyanins from berries has a beneficial effect on cardiovascular health and on reducing cancer risk.

While exotic berries such as goji and acai may well have good antioxidant power, there are in fact fantastic benefits from fresh and frozen local berries. Choose from whatever is available near you. Raspberries, blackberries, blueberries, strawberries, and blackcurrants all have varying levels of different beneficial plant chemicals and are worthy of daily inclusion in your diet.

Studies suggest

that pomegranates can improve insulin sensitivity and help to control blood glucose levels, assist in improving blood cholesterol profiles, and exert an anti-inflammatory effect. All told, it really is worth the effort of removing the seeds. Pomegranate works equally well in savory and sweet dishes. Try adding it to your salads, in a marinade for roast meat, or sprinkle it over your muesli.

Rich in antioxidants, strawberries are a great source of vitamin C and fiber. They are also a good source of the trace mineral manganese, which is essential for healthy bone structure.

lemon cakes with roasted strawberries

⅔ cup almonds

⅔ cup whole-wheat (all-purpose) spelt flour

2 eggs

⅓ cup low-GI caster (superfine) sugar (see tip)

¼ cup brown rice syrup

3 teaspoons finely grated lemon zest

2 tablespoons extra-virgin olive oil

2 tablespoons lemon juice

½ teaspoon baking powder

roasted strawberries

1 pound strawberries, halved

¼ cup honey

1½ tablespoons lemon juice

1 Preheat oven to 350°F. Grease an 8-hole (½-cup) loaf pan. Line base of pan holes with strips of parchment paper, extending the paper 1¼ inches over long sides.
2 Process nuts and 2 teaspoons of the flour until finely ground.
3 Beat eggs, sugar, syrup, and zest in a small bowl with an electric mixer on medium-high speed for 10 minutes or until thick and pale. Reduce speed to low, gradually beat in oil and juice until just combined. Stir in nut mixture, then sifted remaining flour and baking powder; return any husks to bowl. Spoon mixture into holes.
4 Bake cakes for 25 minutes or until a skewer inserted in the center comes out clean. Let cakes stand in pan for 5 minutes, before turning top-side up onto a wire rack to cool.
5 Make roasted strawberries.
6 Serve cakes warm with roasted strawberries.
roasted strawberries Combine ingredients in a medium ovenproof dish. Roast, uncovered, for 10 minutes or until softened. Stir gently. Stand 5 minutes.

prep + cook time 1 hour (+ standing) **makes** 8
nutritional count per cake 13.8g total fat (1.6g saturated fat); 306 cal; 37.7g carbohydrate; 7g protein; 3.5g fiber

tip You can also use coconut sugar or agave for this recipe.

serving suggestion Serve with Greek-style yogurt.

Parfait means "perfect" in French and there's a lot about this dessert that's perfect. For starters, it's easy to make and doesn't melt too quickly which means it's great for entertaining. It's also packed with valuable antioxidant-rich berries.

chocolate, honey, and red berry parfait

You will need to start this recipe a day ahead.

½ cup almonds

1 vanilla bean

12½ ounces ricotta

⅔ cup plus 2 tablespoons honey

2 cups Greek-style yogurt

3 ounces dark chocolate (70% cocoa), chopped

3 ounces raspberries

3 ounces cherries, halved, pitted

1 Preheat oven to 350°F. Line the base of a 4-inch x 9½-inch terrine or loaf pan with parchment paper, extending the paper over two long sides.

2 Spread nuts in a single layer on a baking sheet. Roast nuts for 10 minutes or until skins begin to split. Cool. Chop nuts coarsely.

3 Meanwhile, split vanilla bean lengthwise; scrape seeds into a food processor. Add ricotta and ⅔ cup honey; process until smooth. Transfer mixture to a large bowl.

4 Fold in chopped nuts, yogurt, chocolate, raspberries, and cherries. Spoon mixture into pan; smooth top. Cover with foil. Freeze for 8 hours or overnight until firm.

5 Wipe base and sides of pan with a warm cloth. Turn parfait onto a chopping board; cut into slices. Divide slices among shallow serving dishes. Let stand for 10 minutes before serving, drizzled with 2 tablespoons honey.

prep + cook time 40 minutes (+ cooling, freezing & standing)
serves 8
nutritional count per serving 19g total fat (8.8g saturated fat); 416 cal; 50g carbohydrate; 12g protein; 2g fiber

tip Cut the parfait with a large straight-bladed knife.

serving suggestion Serve with extra raspberries and cherries.

glossary

allspice also known as pimento or Jamaican pepper; so-named because it tastes like a combination of nutmeg, cumin, clove and cinnamon. Available whole or ground.

almonds flat, pointy-tipped creamy white kernel with a brown skin.

blanched brown skins removed.

sliced paper-thin slices.

baking soda a leavening agent.

barley a nutritious grain used in soups and stews. Hulled barley, the least processed, is high in fiber. Pearl barley has had the husk removed then been steamed and polished so that only the "pearl" of the original grain remains, much the same as white rice.

bay leaves aromatic leaves from the bay tree available fresh or dried; adds a strong, slightly peppery flavor.

beans

borlotti also called roman beans or pink beans, can be eaten fresh or dried. Interchangeable with pinto beans due to their similarity in appearance—pale pink or beige with dark red streaks.

broad (fava) also called windsor and horse beans; available dried, fresh, canned and frozen. Fresh should be peeled twice (discarding the outer long green pod and the beige-green tough inner shell); frozen beans have had their pods removed but the beige shell still needs removal.

cannellini a small white bean similar in appearance and flavor to other white beans (great northern, navy or haricot), all of which can be substituted for the other. Available dried or canned.

kidney medium-sized red bean, slightly floury in texture, yet sweet in flavor.

white a generic term we use for canned or cannellini, haricot, navy or great northern beans belonging to the same family, *phaseolus vulgaris*.

beets also known as red beets; firm, round root vegetable.

bell pepper also called pepper. Comes in many colors: red, green, yellow, orange and purplish-black. Be sure to discard seeds and membranes before use.

bok choy also known as pak choi, Chinese white cabbage, or Chinese chard; has a fresh, mild mustard taste. Use both stems and leaves. Baby bok choy, also known as pak kat farang or shanghai bok choy, is smaller and more tender than bok choy.

breadcrumbs

fresh bread, usually white, processed into crumbs.

panko (Japanese) are available in two kinds: larger pieces and fine crumbs; have a lighter texture than Western-style ones. Available from Asian food stores and most supermarkets.

stale made by grating, blending or processing 1- or 2-day-old bread.

broccolini a cross between broccoli and chinese kale; long asparagus-like stems with a long loose floret, both completely edible. Resembles broccoli but is milder and sweeter in taste.

butter use salted or unsalted (sweet) butter; 125g is equal to one stick of butter (4 ounces).

buttermilk originally the term given to the slightly sour liquid left after butter was churned from cream, today it is made from no-fat or low-fat milk to which specific bacterial cultures have neen added. Despite its name, it is actually low in fat.

capers grey-green buds of a warm climate shrub (usually Mediterranean); sold dried and salted or pickled in a vinegar brine. Rinse before using.

cardamom a spice native to India and used extensively in its cuisine; can be purchased in pod, seed or ground form. Has a distinctive aromatic, sweetly rich flavor.

celeriac (celery root) tuberous root with knobbly brown skin, white flesh and a celery-like flavor. Keep peeled celeriac in acidulated water to stop it discoloring. It can be grated and eaten raw in salads; used in soups and stews; boiled and mashed like potatoes; or sliced thinly and deep-fried as chips.

cheese

feta Greek in origin; a crumbly textured goat- or sheep-milk cheese having a sharp, salty taste. Ripened and stored in salted whey.

feta, Persian a soft, creamy feta marinated in a blend of olive oil, garlic, herbs and spices. It is available from most larger supermarkets.

goat made from goat's milk, has an earthy, strong taste; available in both soft and firm textures, in various shapes and sizes, and sometimes rolled in ash or herbs.

halloumi a firm, cream-colored sheep-milk cheese matured in brine; halloumi can be grilled or fried, briefly, without breaking down. Should be eaten while still warm as it becomes tough and rubbery on cooling.

parmesan also called parmigiano; is a hard, grainy cow-milk cheese originating in Italy. Reggiano is the best variety.

pecorino the Italian generic name for cheeses made from sheep's milk; hard, white to pale-yellow cheeses. If you can't find it, use parmesan.

ricotta a soft, sweet, moist, white cow-milk cheese with a low fat content and a slightly grainy texture. The name roughly translates as "cooked again" and refers to ricotta's manufacture from a whey that is itself a by-product of other cheese making.

chickpeas (garbanzo beans) an irregularly round, sandy-colored legume. Firm texture even after cooking, a floury mouth-feel and robust nutty flavor; available canned or dried (reconstitute for several hours in cold water before use).

chile use rubber gloves when seeding and chopping fresh chilees as they can burn your skin. Removing membranes and seeds lessens the heat level.

long available both fresh and dried; a generic term used for any moderately hot, thin, long (6-8cm/2¼-3¼ inch) chile.

Chinese cooking wine (shao hsing) also known as chinese rice wine; made from fermented rice, wheat, sugar and salt with a 13.5% alcohol content. Inexpensive and found in Asian food shops; if you can't find it, replace with mirin or sherry.

Chinese five-spice powder a fragrant mixture of ground cinnamon, cloves, star anise, sichuan pepper and fennel seeds.

choy sum also known as pakaukeo or flowering cabbage, a member of the bok choy family; easy to identify with its long stems, light green leaves and yellow flowers. Stems and leaves are edible.

cinnamon available in sticks (quills) and ground into powder; used as a sweet, fragrant flavoring in sweet and savoury foods.

cocoa powder also known as cocoa; dried, unsweetened, roasted and ground cocoa beans (cacao seeds).

dutch-processed is treated with an alkali to neutralize its acids. It has a reddish-brown color, a mild flavor and easily dissolves in liquids.

coconut

flaked dried flaked coconut flesh.

milk not the liquid found inside the fruit (coconut water), but the diluted liquid from the second pressing of the white flesh of a mature coconut (the first pressing produces coconut cream).

cilantro also known as pak chee or chinese parsley; a bright-green leafy herb with a pungent flavor. Both the stems and roots of cilantro are also used in cooking; wash well before using. Also available ground or as seeds; these should not be substituted for fresh cilantro as the tastes are completely different.

couscous a fine, grain-like cereal product made from semolina; it swells to three or four times its original size when liquid is added.

cumin also known as zeera or comino; has a spicy, nutty flavor.

dukkah an Egyptian specialty spice mixture made up of roasted nuts, seeds and an array of aromatic spices.

edamame (shelled soy beans) available frozen from Asian food stores and some supermarkets.

eggplant also known as aubergine. Ranging in size from tiny to very large and in color from pale green to deep purple.

fennel also known as finocchio or anise; a white to very pale green-white, firm, crisp, roundish vegetable about 8-12cm in diameter. The bulb has a slightly sweet, anise flavor but the leaves have a much stronger taste. Also the name given to dried seeds having a licorice flavor.

fish sauce called naam pla (Thai) and nuoc naam (Vietnamese); the two are almost identical. Made from pulverised salted fermented fish (often anchovies); has a pungent smell and strong taste. Available in varying degrees of intensity, so use according to your taste.

flour

chickpea (besan) made from ground chickpeas so is gluten-free and high in protein. Used in Indian cooking.

plain (all-purpose) an all-purpose wheat flour.

self-rising plain flour sifted with baking powder in the proportion of 1 cup flour to 2 teaspoons baking powder.

wholemeal also known as whole-wheat flour; milled with the wheat germ so is higher in fiber and more nutritional than plain flour.

gai lan also known as chinese broccoli, gai larn, kanah, gai lum and chinese kale; appreciated more for its stems than its coarse leaves.

ginger, pickled pink or red in color, paper-thin shavings of ginger pickled in a mixture of vinegar, sugar and natural coloring. Available from Asian food shops.

kaffir lime leaves also known as bai magrood. Aromatic leaves of a citrus tree; two glossy dark green leaves joined end to end, forming a rounded hourglass shape. A strip of fresh lime peel may be substituted for each kaffir lime leaf.

kecap manis a thick soy sauce with added sugar and spices. The sweetness is derived from the addition of molasses or palm sugar.

labne is a soft cheese made by salting plain (natural) yogurt and draining it of whey for up to 2 days until it becomes thick enough to roll into small balls, which may be scattered with or rolled in chopped herbs or spices.

leeks a member of the onion family, the leek resembles a green onion but is much larger and more subtle in flavor. Tender baby or pencil leeks can be eaten whole with minimal cooking but adult leeks are usually trimmed of most of the green tops then chopped or sliced.

lentils (red, brown, yellow) dried pulses often identified by and named after their color; also known as dhal.

French-style green are a local cousin to the famous French lentils du puy; green-blue, tiny lentils with a nutty, earthy flavor and a hardy nature that allows them to be rapidly cooked without disintegrating.

maple syrup, pure distilled from the sap of sugar maple trees found only in Canada and the USA. Maple-flavored syrup or pancake syrup is not an adequate substitute for the real thing.

miso fermented soybean paste. There are many types of miso, each with its own aroma, flavor, color and texture; it can be kept, airtight, for up to a year in the fridge. Generally, the darker the miso, the saltier the taste and denser the texture. Salt-reduced miso is available. Buy in tubs or plastic packs.

mushrooms

enoki clumps of long, spaghetti-like stems with tiny, snowy white caps.

flat large, flat mushrooms with a rich earthy flavor. They are sometimes misnamed field mushrooms, which are wild mushrooms.

oyster also known as abalone; grey-white mushroom shaped like a fan. Prized for their smooth texture and subtle, oyster-like flavor.

shiitake when fresh are also called chinese black, forest or golden oak mushrooms; although cultivated, they are large and meaty and have the earthiness and taste of wild mushrooms. When dried, they are called donko or dried chinese mushrooms; rehydrate before use.

swiss brown also known as cremini or roman mushrooms, are light brown mushrooms having a full-bodied flavor.

muslin inexpensive, undyed, finely woven cotton fabric called for in cooking to strain stocks and sauces; if unavailable, use disposable coffee filter papers.

mustard seeds are available in black, brown or yellow varieties. They are available from major supermarkets and health-food shops.

noodles, soba thin, pale-brown noodle originally from Japan; made from buckwheat and varying proportions of wheat flour. Available dried and fresh and flavored.

oil

cooking spray we use a cholesterol-free spray made from canola oil.

olive made from ripened olives. Extra-virgin and virgin are the first and second press, respectively, of the olives and are therefore considered the best; the "extra light" or "light" name on other types refers to taste not fat levels.

peanut pressed from ground peanuts; has a high smoke point (capacity to handle high heat without burning).

sesame made from roasted, crushed, white sesame seeds; used as a flavoring rather than a cooking medium.

onions

green (scallions) also known as, incorrectly, shallot; an immature onion picked before the bulb has formed. Has a long, bright-green edible stalk.

red also known as spanish, red spanish or bermuda onion; a sweet-flavored, large, purple-red onion.

shallots also called french shallots, golden shallots or eschalots; small, brown-skinned, elongated members of the onion family.

orange sweet potato also known as kumara, the Polynesian name of an orange-fleshed sweet potato often confused with yam.

parchment paper also called baking parchment—is a silicone-coated paper that is primarily used for lining baking pans and baking sheets so cooked food doesn't stick, making removal easy.

pepitas (pumpkin seeds) are the pale green kernels of dried pumpkin seeds; they can be bought plain or salted.

pine nuts not a nut but a small, cream-colored kernel from pine cones. They are best roasted before use to bring out the flavor.

pomegranate dark-red, leathery-skinned fresh fruit about the size of an orange filled with hundreds of seeds, each wrapped in an edible lucent-crimson pulp having a unique tangy sweet-sour flavor.

pomegranate molasses not to be confused with pomegranate syrup or grenadine; pomegranate molasses is thicker, browner and more concentrated in flavor—tart, sharp, slightly sweet and fruity. Available from Middle Eastern food stores or specialty food shops.

quinoa pronounced keen-wa; is a gluten-free grain. It has a delicate, slightly nutty taste and chewy texture.

radicchio a red-leafed Italian chicory with a refreshing bitter taste that's eaten raw and grilled. Comes in varieties named after their places of origin, such as round-headed verona or long-headed treviso.

rice

basmati a white, fragrant long-grained rice. Wash several times before cooking.

jasmine fragrant long-grained rice; white rice can be substituted, but will not taste the same.

roasting/toasting nuts and dried coconut can be roasted in the oven to restore their fresh flavor and release their aromatic essential oils. Spread them evenly onto a baking sheet then roast at 180°C/350°F for about 5 minutes. Desiccated coconut, pine nuts and sesame seeds roast more evenly if stirred over low heat in a heavy-based frying pan; their natural oils will help turn them golden brown.

saffron available ground or in strands; imparts a yellow-orange color to food once infused. The quality can vary greatly; the best is the most expensive spice in the world.

snow peas also called mange tout (eat all). Snow pea tendrils, the growing shoots of the plant, are also available at greengrocers.

sprouts are the tender new growths of snow peas.

soy sauce made from fermented soya beans. Several variations are available in most supermarkets and Asian food stores. We use japanese soy sauce unless otherwise indicated.

spinach also known as english spinach and, incorrectly, silver beet. Baby spinach leaves are best eaten raw in salads; the larger leaves should be added last to soups, stews and stir-fries, and should be cooked until barely wilted.

sugar

brown very soft, finely granulated sugar retaining molasses for its characteristic color and flavor.

caster (superfine) finely granulated table sugar.

palm also called nam tan pip, jaggery, jawa or gula melaka; made from the sap of the sugar palm tree. Light brown to black in color and usually sold in rock-hard cakes; use with brown sugar if unavailable.

sumac a purple-red, astringent spice ground from berries growing on shrubs that flourish wild around the mediterranean; adds a tart, lemony flavor to food. Available from spice shops and major supermarkets.

tahini a rich, sesame-seed paste, used in most Middle-Eastern cuisines, especially Lebanese, in dips and sauces.

tamazest the tamazest tree produces clusters of hairy brown pods, each of which is filled with seeds and a viscous pulp, that are dried and pressed into the blocks of tamazest found in Asian food shops. Gives a sweet-sour, slightly astringent taste to marinades, sauces, and dressings.

tomato

canned whole peeled tomatoes in natural juices; available crushed, chopped or diced. Use undrained.

paste triple-concentrated tomato puree used to flavor soups, stews and sauces.

truss small vine-ripened tomatoes with vine still attached.

turmeric also called kamin; is a rhizome related to galangal and ginger. Must be grated or pounded to release its acrid aroma and pungent flavor. Known for the golden color it imparts, fresh turmeric can be substituted with the more commonly found dried powder.

vanilla

bean dried, long, thin pod from a tropical golden orchid; the minuscule black seeds inside the bean impart a luscious flavor.

extract obtained from vanilla beans infused in water; a non-alcoholic version of essence.

vinegar

balsamic originally from Modena, Italy, there are now many balsamic vinegars on the market ranging in pungency and quality depending on how, and for how long, they have been aged. Quality can be determined up to a point by price; use the most expensive sparingly.

white balsamic is a clear and lighter version of balsamic vinegar; it has a fresh, sweet, clean taste.

water chestnut resembles a chestnut in appearance, hence the English name. They are small brown tubers with a crisp, white, nutty-tasting flesh. Their crunchy texture is best experienced fresh, however, canned water chestnuts are more easily obtained.

watercress one of the cress family, a large group of peppery greens. Highly perishable, so must be used as soon as possible after purchase.

wombok (napa cabbage) also known as peking cabbage, chinese cabbage or petsai; elongated in shape with pale green, crinkly leaves.

wrappers, gow gee made of flour, egg and water, are found in the refrigerated or freezer section of Asian food stores and supermarkets. These come in different thicknesses and shapes. Thin wrappers work best in soups, while the thicker ones are best for frying.

yeast (dried and fresh), a raising agent used in dough making. Granular (7g sachets) and fresh compressed (20g blocks) yeast can almost always be substituted for the other.

yogurt, Greek-style plain yogurt strained in a cloth (traditionally muslin) to remove the whey and to give it a creamy consistency.

index

A

alliums 123
almonds 61
  miso almond veggie patties 42
  pasta with almond and walnut paste,
    pears and fava beans 74
apple, cherry and rosemary crumble
  213
avocado 103
  chilled avocado soup with crab 116
  kidney bean, onion and arugula
    frittatas with avocado dressing 16
  pesto with shrimp and pasta 119

B

beef
  korean steak tacos with pickled
    vegetables 177
  napa cabbage and herb salad with beef
    and tamazest dressing 96
  steak with cashew nam jim and
    asian greens 209
  warm beef salad with black-eyed peas,
    corn and chimichurri 186
beet
  roast beet, garlic, and chia seed tart
    135
  venison with baby beet salad and
    raspberry vinaigrette 189
bell pepper 131
  spelt pasta with braised bell pepper,
    nuts and chile 69
berries 229
  chocolate, honey and red berry
    parfait 233
  lemon cakes with roasted strawberries
    230
  poached pear and blueberries 225
brassicas 115
bread, seeded pumpkin 54
bream with kohlrabi, watercress
  and walnut salad with buttermilk
  dressing 171
broccoli and ocean trout salad 132

C

cabbage
  napa cabbage and herb salad with
    beef and tamazest dressing 96

pickled cabbage salad 42
  seeded carrot and cabbage filo pie 128
cashews 61
  coconut-roasted pumpkin and
    cauliflower with chile, lime and, 88
  nam jim 209
cauliflower
  cauliflower and tomato gratin 124
  coconut-roasted pumpkin and
    cauliflower with chile, lime and
    cashews 88
  grilled quail with cauliflower
    and pomegranate salad 182
  spiced chickpea and cauliflower dosa 46
chard risotto 99
chicken 201
  coconut-cilantro chicken and
    vegetable curry 202
  roast with fava beans and lemon 178
  small chickens (spatchcock) 185
  white cooked, with ginger rice 194
chickpeas
  chickpea, barley, orange and cherry
    salad 53
  mussels, sweet potato, chickpeas and
    greens in korma sauce 163
  roast sweet potato and pear salad with
    crunchy chickpeas 84
  spiced chickpea and cauliflower dosa 46
  vegetable harira soup 57
chile 131
  coconut-roasted pumpkin and
    cauliflower with chile, lime and
    cashews 88
  spelt pasta with braised bell pepper,
    nuts and chile 69
  sumac chile lamb 197
chocolate 217
  chocolate, honey and red berry
    parfait 233
  dark chocolate and ricotta mousse 218
  ricotta and chocolate cheesecake
    with grapes 226
citrus fruits 221
clams 151 see also seafood
cocoa 217
coconut, cilantro chicken and
  vegetable curry 202
coconut-roasted pumpkin and cauliflower
  with chile, lime and cashews 88
curry
  coconut, cilantro chicken and
    vegetable 202
  sweet potato, eggplant and coconut 120

D

dairy food 19 see also yogurt
dressing 32, 88, 132, 168, 189
  buttermilk 171
  creamy zucchini 79
  spicy 80
  tamazest 96
dumplings, spinach and ginger 80

E

eggplant
  sweet potato, eggplant and coconut
    curry 120
  romesco sauce with eggplant and
    zucchini 58
eggs 27
  fried eggs and spiced yogurt sauce 11
  huevos rancheros 28
  kidney bean, onion and arugula
    frittatas with avocado dressing 16
  mushroom, tomato and goat cheese
    omelets 31
  poached eggs, portobello mushrooms
    and spinach with sweet potato rösti 12
  shrimp, pea and fava bean frittata
    with lemon herb salad 152
  soft-boiled egg and brown rice
    nasi goreng 20

F

fava beans
  pasta with almond and walnut paste,
    pears and fava beans 74
  roast chicken with fava beans and
    lemon 178
  shrimp, pea and fava bean frittata
    with lemon herb salad 152
fennel
  grilled sardines with fennel and
    preserved lemon 172
  pea, fennel and spinach lasagne 107
  pork and fennel ragù with sweet potato
    and goat cheese gnocchi 205
fish 167 see also seafood
five spice pork fillet 198
freekeh 73
  spiced freekeh with cucumber and
    garlic minted yogurt 65
french toast with poached cherries 24

frittata/s
kidney bean, onion and arugula, with avocado dressing 16
shrimp, pea and fava bean frittata with lemon herb salad 152

G

gai lan, sichuan 100
garlic 123
grains 73 *see also* rice
chickpea, barley, orange and cherry salad 53
french toast with poached cherries 24
mediterranean grain salad with honey cumin labne 70
muesli with poached pears and sheep's milk yogurt 62
rosemary and tomato barley risotto with mozzarella 45
seeded pumpkin bread 54
spelt crêpes with poached pears and blueberries 225
spelt pasta with braised bell pepper, nuts and chile 69
spelt pizza with sweet potato, pepitas and goat cheese 66
spelt spaghetti with cherry tomato sauce and clams 111
spiced freekeh with cucumber and garlic minted yogurt 65
Greek-style lamb bolognese 181

H

harissa and tomato shrimp with feta 144
honey and lime baked persimmons 222
huevos rancheros 28

K

kale 83
salad with creamy zucchini dressing 79
whiting with pine nuts, currants and lacinato kale 164
kidney bean, onion and arugula frittatas with avocado dressing 16

L

labne 32
labne and tomato salad with seeds 32
mediterranean grain salad with honey cumin labne 70
lamb
bolognese, Greek-style 181
spicy roast pumpkin with 127
sumac chile 197
wraps with red salad and harissa yogurt 206
lasagne, pea, fennel and spinach 107
leafy greens 83

lean red meat 193
lemon cakes with roasted strawberries 230
lime and cardamom sheep's milk yogurt with tropical fruit 15

M

mediterranean grain salad with honey cumin labne 70
miso almond veggie patties 42
mousse, dark chocolate and ricotta 218
muesli with poached pears and sheep's milk yogurt 62
mushrooms
mushroom, tomato and goat cheese omelets 31
poached eggs, portobello mushrooms and spinach with sweet potato rösti 12
mussels 151
mussels, sweet potato, chickpeas and greens in korma sauce 163

N

napa cabbage and herb salad with beef and tamazest dressing 96
nuts 61
cashew nam jim 209
coconut-roasted pumpkin and cauliflower with chile, lime and cashews 88
miso almond veggie patties 42
pasta with almond and walnut paste, pears and fava beans 74
romesco sauce with eggplant and zucchini 58
spelt pasta with braised bell pepper, nuts and chile 69
winter vegetable sauté with prosciutto and hazelnuts 92

O

octopus 159
oils 103
omelets, mushroom, tomato and goat cheese 31
orange and lemon yogurt cups 214
oysters 151
cucumber and shallot salad, with 147

P

pasta
almond and walnut paste, pears and fava beans, with 74
avocado pesto with shrimp and 119
pea, fennel and spinach lasagne 107
spelt spaghetti with cherry tomato sauce and clams 111
spelt, with braised bell pepper, nuts and chile 69

spinach and broccolini pasta with arugula and walnut pesto 95
pea, fennel and spinach lasagne 107
pepitas 49
pumpkin seed pesto 139
spelt pizza with sweet potato, pepitas and goat cheese 66
persimmons, honey and lime baked 222
pizza, spelt, with sweet potato, pepitas and goat cheese 66
pork 201
five spice pork fillet 198
pork and fennel ragù with sweet potato and goat cheese gnocchi 205
poultry 201
pulses 41
chickpea, barley, orange and cherry salad 53
kidney bean, onion and arugula frittatas with avocado dressing 16
mussels, sweet potato, chickpeas and greens in korma sauce 163
roasted tomato and white bean soup 112
spiced chickpea and cauliflower dosa 46
spicy white bean panzanella 38
vegetable harira soup 57
warm beef salad with black-eyed peas, corn and chimichurri 186
white bean puree 197
pumpkin
coconut-roasted pumpkin and cauliflower with chile, lime and cashews 88
seeded pumpkin bread 54
spicy roast pumpkin with lamb 127
stir-fried pumpkin, water spinach and tomatoes with five spice 108

Q

quail 185
grilled with cauliflower and pomegranate salad 182
quinoa 49
indian-spiced quinoa cakes with tomatoes 50
salad with halloumi and pomegranate 37

R

red meat, lean 193
rice
chard risotto 99
ginger 194
fig and brown rice pilaf 190
seared wasabi salmon and brown rice salad 140
soft-boiled egg and brown rice nasi goreng 20
ricotta and chocolate cheesecake with grapes 226

ricotta, baked, with grilled vegetables and salsa verde 23
romesco sauce with eggplant and zucchini 58
rosemary and tomato barley risotto with mozzarella 45

S

salad
 bream with kohlrabi, watercress and walnut salad with buttermilk dressing 171
 broccoli and ocean trout 132
 chickpea, barley, orange and cherry salad 53
 grilled quail with cauliflower and pomegranate 182
 kale salad with creamy zucchini dressing 79
 labne and tomato salad with seeds 32
 mediterranean grain salad with honey cumin labne 70
 napa cabbage and herb salad with beef and tamazest dressing 96
 quinoa salad with halloumi and pomegranate 37
 roast sweet potato and pear salad with crunchy chickpeas 84
 seared wasabi salmon and brown rice 140
 spicy white bean panzanella 38
 vegetable larb 104
 venison with baby beet salad and raspberry vinaigrette 189
 warm beef salad with black-eyed peas, corn and chimichurri 186
salmon 143
 baked salmon fillets with tahini sauce and tabbouleh 148
 salmon and zucchini burgers with green hummus 155
 seared wasabi salmon and brown rice salad 140
seafood 143 see also mussels; prawns; salmon
 baked baby barramundi with pumpkin seed pesto 139
 baked sardines with fig and pine nut stuffing 160
 bream with kohlrabi, watercress and walnut salad with buttermilk dressing 171
 broccoli and ocean trout salad 132
 chilled avocado soup with crab 116
 grilled sardines with fennel and preserved lemon 172
 harissa and tomato shrimp with feta 144
 oysters with cucumber and shallot salad 147
 small fish 167
 snapper and bay leaf skewers with root vegetable slaw 156

spelt spaghetti with cherry tomato sauce and clams 111
whiting with pine nuts, currants and lacinato kale 164
seeds 49
 indian-spiced quinoa cakes with tomatoes 50
 labne and tomato salad with seeds 32
 muesli with poached pears and sheep's milk yogurt 62
 quinoa salad with halloumi and pomegranate 37
 roast beet, garlic and chia seed tart 135
 seeded carrot and cabbage filo pie 128
 seeded pumpkin bread 54
shellfish 151
shrimp 159
 harissa and tomato shrimp with feta 144
 shrimp, pea and fava bean frittata with lemon herb salad 152
 thai shrimp with soba noodles and asparagus 168 sichuan gai lan 100
snapper and bay leaf skewers with root vegetable slaw 156
soup
 chilled avocado soup with crab 116
 roasted tomato and white bean 112
 vegetable harira 57
spatchcock (small chickens) 185
spelt crêpes with poached pear and blueberries 225
spelt pasta with braised bell pepper, nuts and chile 69
spelt pizza with sweet potato, pepitas and goat cheese 66
spelt spaghetti with cherry tomato sauce and clams 111
spiced chickpea and cauliflower dosa 46
spiced freekeh with cucumber and garlic minted yogurt 65
spicy white bean panzanella 38
spinach 83
 pea, fennel and spinach lasagne 107
 poached eggs, portobello mushrooms and spinach with sweet potato rösti 12
 spinach and broccolini pasta with arugula and walnut pesto 95
 spinach and ginger dumplings 80
steak see beef
stir-fried pumpkin, water spinach and tomatoes with five spice 108
sumac chile lamb 197
sweet potato
 mussels, sweet potato, chickpeas and greens in korma sauce 163
 poached eggs, flat mushrooms and spinach with sweet potato rösti 12
 roast sweet potato and pear salad with crunchy chickpeas 84
 spelt pizza with sweet potato, pepitas and goat cheese 66
 sweet potato and goat cheese gnocchi 205

sweet potato, eggplant and coconut curry 120

T

tomato
 cauliflower and tomato gratin 124
 labne and tomato salad with seeds 32
 mushroom, tomato and goat cheese omelets 31
 roasted tomato and white bean soup 112
 rosemary and barley risotto with mozzarella 45
 stir-fried pumpkin, water spinach and tomatoes with five spice 108
turkey koftas with fig and brown rice pilaf 190

V

vegetable harira soup 57
vegetable larb 104
vegetable, tofu and noodle broth, japanese-style 87
venison with baby beet salad and raspberry vinaigrette 189

W

walnuts 61
 pasta with almond and walnut paste, pears and fava beans 74
white meats 201
whiting with pine nuts, currants and lacinato kale 164
winter vegetable sauté with prosciutto and hazelnuts 92

Y

yogurt 19
 cucumber yogurt 46
 fried eggs and spiced yogurt sauce 11
 garlic minted yogurt 65
 lamb wraps with red salad and harissa yogurt 206
 lime and cardamom sheep's milk yogurt with tropical fruit 15
 muesli with poached pears and sheep's milk yogurt 62
 orange and lemon yogurt cups 214

Z

zucchini
 creamy zucchini dressing 79
 romesco sauce with eggplant and zucchini 58
 salmon and zucchini burgers with green hummus 155

weldon**owen**

Published in the United States by Weldon Owen
1045 Sansome Street, San Francisco, CA 94111
www.weldonowen.com
Weldon Owen is a division of Bonnier Publishing USA

This edition published in arrangement with Bauer Media Pty Limited.
First published in Australia in 2014 by Bauer Media Pty Limited under
the title *Superfoods: Everyday Foods with Super-Nutritional Benefits to
Boost Your Health.* © Bauer Media Pty Limited 2015. All rights reserved.

ISBN 978-1-68188-376-2

Library of Congress Cataloging-in-Publication data is available

Printed and bound in China

This edition printed in 2017

10 9 8 7 6 5 4 3 2 1